国际学术会议交流英语
English for International Academic Conferences and Exchanges

甘小亚 李 静 邹 丽 编著

苏州大学出版社

图书在版编目(CIP)数据

国际学术会议交流英语 / 甘小亚,李静,邹丽编著
. —苏州:苏州大学出版社,2023.2(2024.9重印)
ISBN 978-7-5672-4106-0

Ⅰ.①国… Ⅱ.①甘…②李…③邹… Ⅲ.①国际学术会议-英语 Ⅳ.①H31

中国版本图书馆 CIP 数据核字(2022)第 257122 号

书　　名:	国际学术会议交流英语 English for International Academic Conferences and Exchanges
编　　著:	甘小亚　李　静　邹　丽
责任编辑:	汤定军
策划编辑:	汤定军
封面设计:	吴　钰
出版发行:	苏州大学出版社(Soochow University Press)
社　　址:	苏州市十梓街1号　邮编:215006
印　　装:	江苏凤凰数码印务有限公司
网　　址:	www.sudapress.com
邮　　箱:	sdcbs@suda.edu.cn
邮购热线:	0512-67480030
销售热线:	0512-67481020
开　　本:	787 mm×1 092 mm　1/16　印张:12.5　字数:297千
版　　次:	2023年2月第1版
印　　次:	2024年9月第2次印刷
书　　号:	ISBN 978-7-5672-4106-0
定　　价:	48.00元

凡购本社图书发现印装错误,请与本社联系调换。服务热线:0512-67481020

PREFACE

Globalization has promoted increasing international exchanges in a wide range of areas, and the academic exchange is one of them. Actually, most of the international academic exchanges are conducted by means of academic conferences, which can gather together related experts, scholars, postgraduate students and other researchers from all over the world. The academic conference participants with different work and research experiences will share and discuss on the development path of a certain technique or discipline, its hot issues, research trends and fresh proposals, which often creates inspiring or innovative viewpoints. Admittedly, the academic conference positions as an incubator for academic innovation and progress. Then it is a must for each postgraduate student or research worker to be equipped with the academic conference exchange capability.

Graduate students are the rising force in academics and the backbone of international academic exchange activities. Hence, developing graduate students' academic exchange capability is not only the premise of international academic exchange, but also a necessity of China's technology strategy. As early as in 1993, the postgraduate work committee of the State Education Ministry issued *The Postgraduate English Syllabus for Doctor and Master Candidates*, which clearly stated: "The goal of the postgraduate English teaching is to develop students' ability to use the tool of English to conduct professional study, research and international exchange." Thus, under the context of increasingly frequent academic exchanges, cultivating students' international academic exchange capability is an urgent task.

So far, some relevant works on international academic conference exchanges have been published, including Professor Hu Gengshen's *English on International Conference Exchange*, Professor Cong Cong's *Academic Exchange English Course*, Professor Jia Weiguo's *International Academic English Exchange*, etc., all of which serve to cultivate graduate students' academic communication English capability, and to provide valuable guidance and reference for teachers and students. Inspired by the researchers and teachers' books and papers, we team members venture to comb the ten-year postgraduate English teaching experiences and write this book, expecting to share with nation-wide colleagues and scholars, and to further enhance postgraduates' academic English exchange capability.

This book makes two fresh attempts. Firstly, based on full surveys and analysis, we team members have accordingly determined the book content. This book covers the issues and points that students feel most interesting or difficult in academic conference exchange activities, such as what are the differences between academic conferences and other types of meetings, what is the normal process of an international academic conference, how to communicate with the conference staff in written and spoken ways, how to make presentations or raise questions to the speakers, and so on. All the covered issues and points are based on students' feedback and well matched with their realistic demand. Secondly, with reference to related books, we team members have designed various drilling tasks, which enable students to practice and then improve the language skills and communication skills. Besides, the drilling tasks also improve students' capabilities in autonomy learning, cooperation and critical thinking, all of which help to build their confidence and fluency in international academic exchanges.

The book consists of four parts: (1) the international academic conference features, the conference process and the conference announcements; (2) preconference correspondence with the conference staff; (3) in-conference oral communication; (4) simulated international academic conferences. Each part contains detailed information and drilling tasks. The whole book portrays the whole process of an international academic conference, with a combination of theory and practice, and also a combination of English reading, writing, speaking and listening skills training. Following the book instructions, students can not only improve their academic English reading, writing, speaking and listening skills, but also enhance their autonomy, cooperation and critical thinking.

Features of this book can be summarized as:

1. Pertinence

This book aims to develop postgraduates' international academic exchange capability. Based on full surveys and interview, we determine the book content which echoes with students' interests and difficulties in international academic exchange activities. In addition to the content, the samples in the book are also carefully selected conference-related documents, many of which are shared by professors, researchers and senior postgraduate students with academic conference exchange experiences. Also, various drilling tasks in this book such as drills of comprehension, analysis and comparison are all oriented to the content and aimed to enhance students' academic exchange capability.

2. Comprehensiveness

This book weaves the different stages of an international academic conference into a whole picture. It starts from the preparation for the conference, the correspondence before the conference, the oral communication in the conference, the conference closure, to preparation for a simulated international academic conference, hence students can be acquainted with the whole process of academic conference communication and be confident in the future academic exchange activities.

Simultaneously, this book aims to develop students' academic English capability comprehensively from 4 aspects: reading, writing, speaking and listening. To get acquainted with the academic conference features, conference process and the conference announcement, students will read large amounts of conference documents, improve their mastery of academic and professional terms and sentence patterns, and make acquaintance of conference documents styles and structures. Similarly, in conference correspondence, students will master the basic format and writing skills of various academic letters or emails so as to communicate accurately and appropriately with the conference staff. In conference oral communication activities, students practice orally a lot and then become familiar with the discourse models of different conference speeches and commonly used sentence patterns and expressions in academic oral communication, and accordingly their academic speaking and listening abilities are enhanced. Moreover, various drilling tasks build students' autonomy, cooperation and critical thinking and help to create the image of confident and fluent Chinese scholars in international academic exchange activities.

3. Practicality

This book puts theory into practice. Each chapter includes basic concepts, practical techniques and first-hand academic speech texts while little professional linguistic theories are covered.

In consideration of the practicality of the academic exchange ability, and the inadequacy of drilling designs in related books, this book contains varieties of drills, comprehensive and vivid, to help students to comprehend, analyze, compare and practice, so as to deepen comprehension and improve practical skills. Furthermore, a supplementary part "simulated international academic conference" is provided at the end of the book to review the whole conference process and to assist students to prepare and participate in a mock academic conference. The rehearsal is of great necessity and importance for students to perform fluently and confidently in future actual academic conference.

This book is the outcome of the humanities and social science project of the Education Ministry (21YJA740011) and of the postgraduate teaching quality project of Wuhan University of Science and Technology (Yjg201735). The book can be used as a textbook or a reference book for postgraduate academic conference communication in English, or a reference book for senior undergraduate students with keen interest in international academic exchange, or a reference book for research workers and college teachers.

We, the whole team, have made greatest efforts during the book writing process, expecting to present a good book. We hope the book could assist postgraduates and research workers to achieve fluent, appropriate and confident performance in international academic exchange activities. Due to our limited time and capacity, there still exist errors and mistakes in the book. Hence, we sincerely invite comments and suggestions from every reader. We greatly appreciate the attention, patience and devotion of all readers.

Last but not least, we have made reference to relevant books and websites at home and abroad in the book writing process, and we are most grateful to all the authors of the related materials.

CONTENTS

- **Chapter 1 Basics of International Academic Conferences** / 1
  - Section 1 Various Types of Meetings / 2
  - Section 2 Principal Activities of an International Academic Conference / 9
  - Section 3 Announcement and Agenda of an Academic Conference / 21
  - Section 4 Channels of Obtaining Conference Information / 44
- **Chapter 2 International Academic Conference Correspondence** / 52
  - Section 1 Inquiry About Conference Activities / 53
  - Section 2 Respondence to Conference Invitations / 60
  - Section 3 Correspondence with the Editor / the Paper Reviewer / 69
- **Chapter 3 Delivering Opening and Closing Speeches** / 82
  - Section 1 Delivering Opening Speeches / 83
  - Section 2 Delivering Closing Speeches / 97
  - Section 3 Chairing a Session / 111
- **Chapter 4 Making Presentations** / 118
  - Section 1 Starting and Ending a Speech Presentation / 119
  - Section 2 Developing a Speech Presentation / 131
  - Section 3 Reading Manuscripts Smoothly / 148
- **Chapter 5 Raising and Answering Questions** / 157
  - Section 1 Raising Questions / 159
  - Section 2 Answering Questions / 166
- **Chapter 6 Manners and Etiquette** / 184
- **References** / 190

Basics of International Academic Conferences

International academic conferences are an important channel for postgraduates and research workers to enrich their professional knowledge and vision. The academic communicative capability for postgraduates is like that wings are for birds. Hence students are supposed to be well equipped with relevant knowledge and skills, if they expect the most benefit from the future academic conference communication activities.

This chapter gives a brief introduction to international academic conferences, including the following parts:
- Various types of meetings
- Principal activities of an academic conference
- Academic conference announcements
- Channels of obtaining conference information

Section 1
Various Types of Meetings

Warm-up

Do you know the differences among meeting, forum, rally, conference, convention, workshop, seminar, colloquium, symposium, summit and congress.

Meeting, a widely used word, refers to various kinds of gatherings where people share or discuss certain issues. It can be prearranged or unarranged, formal or informal, large or small-scale, long or short. In this section different meetings will be explained in terms of meaning, usage and context. The following are the most frequently used expressions for meeting.

1. Types of Meetings

(1) **Meeting**

Meeting is a general and summary term of various kinds of assembly of people for a particular purpose. Its original meaning is to "meet with each other", or to "put heads together". In this sense, if there are more than two persons coming together, talking and discussing, the event can be called a meeting. So we can often hear "let's have a meeting". Since the definition of meeting is rather extended and not clearly demarcated, it can mean any kind of gathering, pre-arranged or non-arranged, formal or informal, long or short; the scale, large or small; the number of participants, big or small, and so on. Therefore, the names of meeting should be further specified to clarify a meeting.

(2) **Conference**

Conference, which often lasts for a few days, is organized on a particular subject or to bring together people who have a common interest. Usually, formal discussions take place at a conference.

Comparatively, conference is a rather formal term for meeting, which generally refers to a specialized professional or academic event, e. g. Forbes Global CEO Conference, International Conference on Information and Communication Technologies and Development, and International Conference on Parallel Data Processing.

Conference can also be a meeting for consultation, e. g. the Chinese People's Political Consultative Conference. It can sometimes be within a short period of time, e. g. press conference and teleconference.

(3) **Symposium**

Symposium is also a kind of meeting, but it refers exclusively to the meeting for specialized academic discussion.

At a symposium, experts, scholars and other participants of a particular field discuss a particular subject. For example, at the First International Symposium on Eco-translatology in 2010, over 60 scholars gathered from different parts of the world and discussed their topics of interest in the field of eco-translatology.

Compared with a conference, a symposium is narrower and more specific in the range of topics. It may be smaller than a conference in terms of the scale because sometimes a conference may include several satellite symposiums to be held simultaneously.

Sometimes a certain kind of meeting can be called a "working conference", not "working symposium". Furthermore, some meetings held by the government for political consultation can be called a "political conference", but not "political symposium".

(4) **Convention**

Convention is a kind of routine meeting, at which a large number of people meet and discuss the business of their organization or political group, e. g. the annual convention of the Labor Union, the biannual convention of the Metal Society, etc.

A convention is regularly organized by a learned society, a professional association, an academic institution or a nongovernmental organization.

(5) **Forum**

Forum is in fact a kind of public meeting, at which people exchange ideas and discuss issues, especially important public issues. Examples of noted forums are World Economic Forum, Bo'ao Forum for Asia, Technology Innovation Forum, etc.

(6) **Seminar**

Seminar is a class-like meeting, where participants discuss a particular topic or subject that is presented by several major speakers.

Different from other kinds of meetings, a seminar has the presentations given by chief speakers, with other participants listening and then joining in discussion. In this sense, a seminar can be taken as a lecture plus discussion—the discussion as a follow-up of the lecture. e. g. "This afternoon we'll have a seminar on the topics presented this morning."

(7) **Workshop**

Workshop is a period of discussion or practical work on a particular subject in which a group of people learn about the subject by sharing their knowledge or experience. It emphasizes interaction and exchange of information among a usually small number of participants. Its distinctive feature lies in its emphasis on practical performance, besides the professional and academic discussions. Hence, many relevant activities such as demonstrations and displays may be arranged in a workshop. For example, "Dr. Linda Smith chaired a workshop on artificial intelligence and software development. I saw there were lots of computers and software developers in that lecture hall this morning."

(8) **Colloquium**

Colloquium is sometimes a formal word for seminar.

A large academic seminar is like a panel discussion, attended by certain invited experts or professionals in a particular field. Participants in the colloquium will express their ideas and opinions about a specific topic.

Other types of meetings, such as summit (meeting of top leaders), assembly (gathering of all the staff) and rally (people's gathering to protest against some law or policy), will not be detailed here since they are not closely related to our topic, academic exchange.

Now please discuss with your partner and fill in the table to differentiate various meetings under the following criteria:

Topics (academic, professional, or public issues)	Attendees (research staff or other groups)	Scale (large or small)	Frequency (regularly or irregularly)
Conference			
Congress			
Symposium			
Convention			
Forum			
Seminar			
Colloquium			

2. International Academic Conferences

The above gives a glimpse of different types of meetings. Then comes the meeting discussed in this book, the international academic conference. This part gives a brief introduction to its features and organization.

International academic conferences, generally speaking, are meetings held to gather together research workers from home and abroad for academic exchange and cooperation. Different from other types of meetings, international academic conferences are authoritative, intellectual and interactive. The participants are mainly researchers, teachers and postgraduates, and among whom are well-known scientists, scholars and professors. International academic conferences appeal to research workers since they can reward the participants with plenty of valuable information, e. g. a global picture of a certain field or discipline and deep insight into existing challenges. However, it's never an easy job to organize an international academic conference.

Organizing an international academic conference is laborious and time-consuming, though rewarding and significant. The organization work normally consists of 3 stages, lasting for more than 1 year: pre-conference stage, conference stage and post-conference stage. During the pre-conference stage, firstly, about 12 months before the conference opening the conference organizing committee will publish the conference announcement on the conference webpage or in professional journals calling for papers on related disciplines or professions. Next, 6 months in advance, the organizing committee will collect papers for technical review. With reference to the reviewers' comment, the committee will decide on acceptance or rejection of each collected paper, and then send formal letters of invitation to the authors. Usually, the conference program is sent together with the invitation letter to the participants 4 months in advance of the conference opening. During the conference-holding period, the attendees from all over the world will gather together at the conference venue, present their research results and exchange academic viewpoints. At the post-conference stage, to be more exact, after the presentation and discussion activities are completed, a short tour is sometimes arranged for the participants, which may be of the local research institutes or of local culturally famous spots. Furthermore, a booklet of participants' contact information may be prepared by the conference organizing committee for the conference attendees to launch future cooperation.

Much effort is made to ensure the conference activities proceed smoothly. The following are the fundamental departments or working staff for an international academic conference.

> **Sponsors and Organizers**

The sponsor of an international academic conference is an institution that initiates the conference and is also the financial supporter of the conference. The organizer, however, is the one who is entrusted by the sponsor to organize the conference. The sponsor might also be the organizer, but usually one institution does not play both roles simultaneously.

> **Organizing Committee**

The organizing committee is set up by the sponsor and the organizer of a conference, in charge of organization and arrangement of all the conference activities. Accordingly, the organizing committee will set up some subcommittees, such as academic committee, secretariat, coordinating committee and other committees to perform related functions.

> **Academic Committee**

The academic committee functions to review, discuss and make judgments on academic-related issues of an academic conference. It is also called "program committee", "scientific committee" or "paper committee".

> **Secretariat**

The secretariat plays a big role in conference administration. It should report to the organizing committee performances of different committees, publish conference announcements, and reply timely to inquiry letters or emails from conference participants.

> **Other Committees**

Other committees may be established according to the scale, form, and purpose of a conference, for instance, "international steering committee", "coordinating committee", "executive committee", "local committee", "advisory panel", "board of honorary officers" and "lady's committee".

Exercises

❶ **Answer the following questions to have a global picture of this chapter.**

(1) What are the different expressions for meeting? What are the similarities and differences among them?

(2) Can you use two or three words to describe the features of the international academic conference?

(3) How can we organize an international academic conference?

(4) What are the various sessions or working staff of an international academic

conference?

❷ **Translate the following expressions into English.**

（1）信息通信技术国际会议

（2）福布斯全球总裁会议

（3）第四届世界妇女大会

（4）中国人民政治协商会议

（5）第一届生态翻译学国际研讨会

（6）全国工会年度例会

（7）博鳌亚洲论坛

（8）武汉本土文化研讨会

❸ **Work with your partner to describe the following meetings in terms of the conference topic, attendee, scale and regularity.**

（1）The International Conference on Computer Technology

（2）The First International Symposium on Intercultural Communication

（3）Biannual Convention of National Labor Union

（4）Bo'ao Forum for Asia

（5）Seminar on Hunan Local Culture Development Strategies

❹ **Read the following posters of international academic conferences, and then describe the conferences.**

SIAM Conference on Mathematical & Computational Issues in the Geosciences 2021

September 18, 2020 | antanriva | Leave a comment

The next edition of the SIAM Conference on Mathematical & Computational Issues in the Geosciences (GS21) will take place on July 21-24, 2021 at Politecnico di Milano, Milan, Italy.

The submission of proposals for mini-symposia is NOW OPEN through the SIAM web site, at https://www.siam.org/conferences/cm/conference/gs21.
The conference aims to stimulate the exchange of ideas among geoscientific modellers, applied mathematicians, statisticians, and other scientists, fostering new research in the mathematical foundations with an impact on geoscience applications. Participation of industrial researchers is highly welcomed and traditionally it forms an important part of this conference.

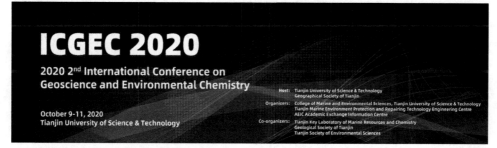

You may use *why*, *what*, *how*, *who*, *when*, *where* to describe it, for example,

- Why are the conferences held?
- What are the themes of the conferences?

- How can we get access to the conferences?
- Who have organized the conferences?
- Who are the conference attendees?
- When and where will the conferences be held?

❺ **Do you think that the above two international academic conferences are authoritative, intellectual and interactive? Why or why not?**

Section 2
Principal Activities of an International Academic Conference

Warm-up

It's never an easy job to hold an international academic conference. The following is the work related to conference preparation. Discuss with your partner about how to deal with the following tasks logically.

◇ determine the conference theme
◇ invite conference sponsors
◇ invite the host, VIPs and potential participants
◇ confirm the attendance of participants
◇ reserve the conference venue, reserve the hotels and conference dinners
◇ plan a site trip to research institutes, factories, or prepare a short tour of cultural interests
◇ arrange the conference receptionists
◇ work out the conference schedule (registration, opening ceremony, welcoming dinner, general assembly, plenary session, parallel session, poster session, closing speech)
◇ contact the speech givers for confirmation of their participation
◇ contact a publishing house to publish the accepted papers
◇ prepare a yellow book for all the participants

Principal activities of international academic conferences vary according to the purpose, the scale and the budget. Normally the following activities will be included in an international academic conference: formal meetings, informal meetings, teaching and consulting services, audio and visual presentations, exhibitions, visits and other social activities.

1. Formal Meetings

Formal meetings usually include the general assembly, the plenary session, the parallel sessions, and the poster session.

(1) **General Assembly**

The general assembly consists of the opening ceremony and the closing ceremony, held at the very beginning and the end of a conference respectively. It is attended by all the conference participants and sometimes by administrative officials as well as reporters. Routinely, in the opening ceremony, relevant administrative officials, conference organizers and distinguished experts or scholars will be invited to deliver opening or welcoming speeches. After the opening or welcoming speech, a group photo is often taken for all the conference participants and conference staff. In the closing ceremony, a closing speech is addressed to declare the success of the conference. Substantial paper presentations are usually not arranged in the general assembly.

(2) **Plenary Session**

The plenary session consists of keynote speeches given by one or more prestigious experts. It means the formal start of academic or professional exchange, normally attended by all the participants, but not including administrative officials. The plenary session of a conference appeals a lot to attendees since they have access to famous experts or scholars' lectures in this session. The invited lectures or keynote presentations by well-known experts of a certain field focus on the themes of the conference and introduce the overall development path or the latest techniques and methodologies. The plenary lectures or presentations take longer time (25 minutes for presentation and 5 minutes for questions and answers) than those allocated for ordinary paper presentations (10 – 12 minutes for presentation and 3 – 5 minutes for questions and answers) in parallel sessions, and are usually followed by questions and discussions as well. Some conferences make clear and strict stipulations for the keynote speeches in order to achieve a satisfying effect, e.g. using fonts not smaller than 20 points, using presentation ratio of 4:3 aspect, 1,024 × 768 resolutions, etc.

(3) Parallel Session

The parallel sessions, as the name implies, refer to smaller-scale meetings held simultaneously, which are therefore also called simultaneous sessions. At these sessions, lecturers present their papers respectively to a group of participants with similar research background. Usually, a special topic is arranged for a particular parallel session, and a large conference has several or dozens of such topics for discussion. For example, in the 1998 IEEE International Symposium on Circuits and Systems held in California, USA, topics discussed in parallel sessions included analog circuits and discrete systems circuit theory and power systems, computer aided design, neural systems, digital signal processing, multimedia, communication systems, computer communication systems, and applications. In the sixth International Pragmatics Conference held in July 1998 in Reims, France, there were such special topics as foreign language teaching and ideological practices, language ideologies vs facts of first- and second-language acquisition communication in cross-cultural perspective, the pragmatics of conflict, negotiation and peace, international communication: theoretical and methodological issues, etc.

In one particular parallel session, participants will present their papers to colleagues with similar research background. Each presenter is normally allotted 15 minutes, with 12 minutes for presentation and 3 minutes for questions and answers. Most conferences give clear stipulations for the presentations in order to achieve a satisfying effect, e. g. using PDF or PPT file to present, with fonts not smaller than 20 points, etc.

(4) Poster Session

The poster session is designed for the participants who intend to present orally but fail to make it because of poor health or other reasons, and for those who are not eligible for oral presentation. In the poster session, papers are posted on boards or walls in a specially separated area of the meeting place, and the participants can read the posted papers and exchange viewpoints with the authors waiting there. In case the author of a posted paper is not around, there may be a small box near the posted paper where the author's name cards are available, or a special place for the audience who want to leave messages to the author. Nowadays, the communication between the participants and the authors has been made much more convenient than before, and some authors put their QR codes at the beginning or the end of the papers to invite the conference participants to whip the codes and exchange opinions in a convenient way. Due to the space limit, the area covered for each paper to be posted is pre-determined by the conference, and the printed materials for display should be clear enough and convenient for distant viewers. Some conferences have kindly provided poster guidelines for authors. The following is a good example:

Poster Presentation Guidelines

The conference format places high importance on poster presentations. The program will include several poster sessions, covering a broad range of climate change relevant topics, to allow ample discussions in a studious, yet relaxed atmosphere. Poster sessions especially facilitate interaction between students / early career scientists and more senior researchers.

Poster Display

Posters should be on display as outlined in the poster session. Posters should be put up just before the scheduled display time and taken off at the very end of the scheduled display time. Authors should be in attendance during the session and are expected to stand by their poster in order to answer questions.

Presenters will be asked to remove their poster at the end of their poster session. The posters not removed during the appropriate time will be recycled. Please DO NOT LAMINATE your poster unless you plan to re-use it. Un-laminated posters can be recycled.

Poster Format

Maximum posters are 118 cm (height) × 84 cm (width) = A0 in PORTRAIT. Poster areas will be equipped with poster boards and material to hang your poster up.

Poster ID

Posters are identified with nomenclature according to the sessions: A1, B2, C3. For example, the following poster ID "A3-P-01" refers to a presentation assigned number 01 in poster session A3.

NOTE: No local poster printing service will be available during the symposium, so please bear in mind to print and bring your poster.

TIPS for Your Poster

The purpose of a poster is to effectively communicate your work to a particular audience. You need your poster to be attention-seeking and convey a clear message that the audience will quickly comprehend.

There are 4 key elements in creating an effective poster:
- Attract interest
- Help your audience navigate the poster
- Give them content worth reading
- Make it easy to comprehend

The presentation must cover the material as cited in the corresponding submitted abstract.

Use the official abstract title as submitted and make it easy to read. Complement the title with a short abstract that conveys your main message and attracts people passing by. Place the title on top of your poster together with the author's names.

Highlight the author's names, e-mails, and address information in case the viewer is interested in contacting you for more information and/or provide a card or handout with your contact details.

Organize your material into sections; give each section a sentence heading summarizing it.

Create an attractive design with lots of white space.

Use the same artistic style throughout your poster.

Limit details that don't contribute directly to your main message.

Eye movement: The movement (pathway) of the eye over the poster should be natural, down the columns from left to right. Size attracts attention. Arrows, pointing hands, numbers, and letters can help clarify the sequence.

Topography:
- Avoid abbreviations, acronyms, and jargon.
- Use a consistent font throughout.
- Use type size that is readable from 2 m away. Title text should be at least 54 pt, headings at least 36 pt, and body text at least 28 pt. Keep the number of text characters in a line between 30 and 70. Consider the spacing between the lines.
- Blank spaces are not a problem. Use space to highlight and shape the main content. Used effectively, blank spaces can help the audience navigate the poster.

If several people gather around your poster, they all should be able to read the text simultaneously.

Use graphics as much as possible to get your message across. Prepare all diagrams or charts neatly and legibly.

Simplicity: Resist the temptation to overload the poster. More material may mean less communication.

Poster No Show

Participants are strongly urged to inform the organizers in case of no-show in sending a mail to icrc-cordex2019@lasg.iap.ac.cn with copy to Catherine Michaut.

Question: What should we pay attention to when displaying posters?

2. Informal Meetings

Informal meetings refer to places or occasions for informal communication among participants. Different conferences may have different arrangements. In some academic conferences, informal meetings include activities of free information exchange, free paper presentation, free communication or "walk in and talk", etc. Informal meetings can supplement to the time limit and insufficient opportunities for information exchange at formal meetings. Many participants take advantage of informal meetings to make inquiries to experts or get acquainted with some famous scholars for future cooperation. Participants can also share and discuss their interesting research issues that are related, but not covered in the conference themes. Hence, participants benefit a lot and some even come up with bright ideas after free communication.

3. Audio and Visual Presentations

Many professional presentations need to take advantage of various audio/visual demonstration tools. The use of overhead projectors, slide projectors, videotapes, short film projectors, poster demonstrations, and other audio and visual aids (e.g., with PowerPoint) has currently become very popular in international conferences. Even "slides sessions" may be arranged in some international conferences.

4. Teaching and Consulting Services

Teaching services in international academic conferences include various types of educational courses, pre-conference institutes, and teaching day for tutoring, tutorial workshop or special tuition and so on. The length of teaching services varies from one or two days to one or two weeks, which is up to the content. These teaching services are classes held by the organizers for participants to access required knowledge, mainly for postgraduates and those who are not very familiar with knowledge or technology covered by the conference. Though not popular in China, teaching services are common and welcome in many foreign countries.

Consulting services refer to discussions or consultations closely related to certain practical issues. Usually, the conference organizational committee will invite experts with rich theoretical background and practical experience to offer the participants face-to-face opportunities of consultations on technique application, new concept interpretation, management, etc.

Participants have to pay extra fees for teaching and consulting services if they intend to attend.

5. Exhibitions

Exhibitions play a part in nearly all the academic conferences. There are three main types of exhibitions—conference exhibitions, scientific exhibitions and trade exhibitions. Conference exhibitions are arranged to introduce the achievements of the conference (or similar previous conferences) with photos or posters. Scientific exhibitions are to display scientific research results such as new equipment, crafts, products as well as books and journals. Trade exhibitions, although closely related to commercial activities, are now widely seen in academic conferences. The reason is that academic conferences are partly or even mostly financed by scientific companies or publishing houses. Therefore, trade exhibitions are arranged during the conference especially by the sponsors to promote the sale of particular scientific or technical products and obtain more market recognition of the enterprises.

6. Visits and Other Social Activities

During the intervals or breaks of an academic conference, some social activities or visits are arranged, for example, visits to famous research institutes, universities or museums, and field trips to manufacturing or mining enterprises and construction sites. Tours of local historical or scenic spots are preferred by the conference participants from other cities or countries. Social events in a conference normally include banquets, parties, visits, short tours, etc. In short, these social events provide the participants an access to friendship and cooperation with one another.

Exercises

❶ Answer the following questions to obtain a global picture of conference principal activities.

(1) What are the principal activities of international academic conferences? What factors will affect the conference principal activities?

(2) What are included in formal meetings? Which session of formal meetings is more likely to see postgraduates' presentation?

(3) What are included at informal meetings?

(4) What are teaching and consulting services? Is there any difference in this session between China and the West?

(5) What are audio and visual presentations?

(6) What are the different types of exhibitions?

(7) Which type of conference activities are you most interested in, and why?

❷ Chinese-English or English-Chinese translation.

大会	QR codes
海报展示	presentation ratio of 4∶3 aspect
全体会议	1,024 × 768 resolutions
教学咨询服务	overhead projectors
主题报告	audio and visual aids
会展	field trips
分组会议	group photo
实地考察	avoid abbreviations, acronyms, and jargon
	use a consistent font throughout

❸ **The following passage is about academic poster making. Complete the passage with appropriate words in the box.**

distilled	comply	distract	succinct
minimal	prior	readability	showcase
generate	librarians	embellish	expulsion
aesthetically	contrasting	downwards	collate

Academic posters, when done effectively, are a _____ and attractive way to _____ your work at conferences and meetings. Unlike oral presentations, your audience may not be static, so clear design and _____ content are all more important. Similar to oral presentations, successful posters can _____ discussion amongst the audience members, therefore it is important to have a clear plan of what to say when standing alongside your poster.

There are many computer programs you can use to create your poster. Many use Microsoft Publisher or PowerPoint. It is important that you are comfortable using these programs as you will likely be doing a lot of editing. If you are not familiar with these programs, _____ that are present in most universities will be able and usually willing to help you out.

It is useful to attend a variety of scientific meetings to _____ ideas on how to create an informative and _____ pleasing poster. The most important concept for the overall design is not to overly _____ the poster with formatting and pictures, as this may _____ from the content. The information should be _____, as in a slide presentation, stating only key points rather than complete sentences.

The color system should have effective _____ backgrounds (e.g. blue and yellow, black and white) to ensure the text is easy to read. The flow of the poster should also be logical and ideally follow a longitudinal algorithm. This should begin with aims and objectives and flow _____ in columns to methods, results, conclusions and finally references. The same format is also adopted when writing scientific abstracts. Once the poster is drafted, it is important to adhere to the instructions provided by the congress you are attempting to submit to. Failure to _____ to guidelines may result in your poster not being considered for a poster award, or perhaps even result in _____ from the meeting altogether.

_____ to submission it is also important to ask as many senior colleagues for feedback on your poster as possible. They will be able to provide feedback on the overall _____ of the poster, including formatting. Preparing your poster one month in advance is sufficient to allow for revisions to be made.

❹ Academic conferences are very good chances for participants to learn from each other. The following is the feedback of a conference participant, including what she has done to prepare for conference attendance, what she has benefited from the experience, etc. Please read the feedback carefully, and then make a conversation with your partner. Suppose one of you was the conference participant mentioned above and the other was going to attend an academic conference and wanted to know more about conference participation.

How to Take Advantage of a Conference for Your Career

From July 25th to 27th, Corteva organized for the first time a conference on New Frontiers in Genetic Evaluation in its Johnston seeds headquarters (Iowa, USA).

Among the 21 speakers, 14 were from academics and 7 from Corteva. Topics covered phenotypic and genetic tools that help us better understand genetic evaluation and would help us to develop better products for our customers in the future. About 250 people from all over the world attended the conference, one third of them being graduate students.

Those 3 days have been extremely rich in knowledge exchange. For example, I really enjoyed June Medford's talk, different from the other talks I used to hear, but how cool it is to be able to grow rice in saline water!

Topics covered ranged from genotype by environment interaction, population genetics, biological models to genome editing. Apart from the talks, we also had the chance to interact with graduate students who shared their works through posters and networking activities.

Attendees also got a chance to visit our lab, greenhouses and demo field. Former research fellow in legacy pioneer, along with *** explained some of the history and development of pioneer elite worldwide germplasm.

Therefore, I think this conference was a success: we invited colleagues from over the world to come to our headquarters, visit our labs and fields, and we share the projects we are working on lately. I feel lucky to work in a company that foster the relationship with academics and let us explore opportunities outside of Corteva. I could start listing all the talks I found interesting but that might not reflect the networking opportunities that happened and the exchange of ideas. Instead, I thought I could share how this conference helped me to reflect on my career and on what I've learned since my graduation as a PhD back in 2011 on how I try to take advantage of those conferences for my career.

I have been with Corteva (pioneer legacy) for the past 7 years and as far as I can remember this is the first year there are so many collaborators in Johnston at the same time. When I joined in 2011, I got the chance to attend two of the Dupont Pioneer Symposia in North America that already fostered our collaborations with academics. During the past 2 years I got invited to speak to a couple of them in Europe and always enjoyed the discussions and networking happening at those events.

While I was sitting at the New Frontiers conference last week in a comfortable space, I remembered the other conferences I got to attend as a graduate student and how I would feel about those: stressed, nervous, trying to make the best out of it (without being sure of what it meant).

My experience is probably different from most of the students in North America. I graduated back in 2011 from Agroparistech in Paris, and during my studies the conferences I attended were located in Europe; I got the chance to present my work through posters and also attend the Maize Genetics Conference who took place in Italy back in 2010. Since I joined Corteva, I got to attend several international conferences, not only as an attendee but also as a speaker.

I don't claim of having found all the answers, but I would like to share some of my experiences:

Before the Conference

- Check the program. For the talks that you are most interested in, do some bibliography, so that you are more familiar with the subject and might make it easy on you to talk to the speakers or ask questions during a session.
- Do you recognize any names from a previous conference or an article you have read? Make sure to keep those names in mind when you are at the conference and go talk to them.
- Send emails to whomever you know that will be at this conference, especially if they are working on a project you are interested in or if you want to have time to network with them. This way you make sure you have time with them. Sometimes you arrive at the conference and there are so many people that you lose tracks of the ones you wanted to approach in the first place.

Give Yourself Daily Objectives

- Still today, when I go to a conference, I give myself an objective to meet 5 new people per day. I am usually not a shy person, but I tend to have the Impostor Syndrome and feel that any question I would ask a professor is probably a silly question. Turns out, up to that day I don't think I did too

bad!
- Every day, try to follow-up on at least one poster or one talk, i. e. talk to the person involved in the project or promise you will follow-up after the conference by sending an email to that colleague.

Meet People
- I think the most important factor in any conference are the people. As soon as you can in your career make sure you meet new people. I agree it can be tiring and it takes a lot of efforts, but even meeting one new person at a conference can be rewarding.
- When I was a graduate student, I always felt impressed to talk to the professors, now that I have been living in the US for 7 years I think it is probably something inhered to my culture, because it is amazing how easy it is to talk to professors from the US universities! If you still don't feel comfortable, talk to grad students from the lab you are interested in, they will know all the projects, and can inform you as much as the professors most of the time!

Follow-up with Your New Network Regularly
- When you are back home, make sure to thank the people you met during the conference, for the nice discussion you shared.
- Check if they are on LinkedIn. It's an easy way to keep in touch and check what they are doing. If you want to connect with them, make sure to add a personalized message so that the person remembers you even more.
- Send personalized emails around the holidays.
- Make sure you contact them again if you are presenting in a conference that might be of interest to them, or if you are traveling for work close to where they are located.

Summary/Conclusion

If I look back at when I was a graduate student, I think that what got me where I am today is my network. I have always liked to be prepared for the future and had my career plan ready probably 2 years before graduating, but that felt through the crack 3 months before graduation. Thanks to the network I had built in public and private sector I was able to get in pioneer for a postdoc. And as of right now I don't regret it, I really enjoy my job at Corteva.

This conference was another great opportunity to increase my network and learn about a lot of interesting projects across universities worldwide.

I am always looking on ways to improve my learnings during those events, so if you have any advice, please shoot them! If you have questions about the Corteva

New Frontiers conference, shoot questions as well!

Below a photo with almost all the speakers (missing ***, ***, *** and *** on that photo) from the conference. I am thankful for all the colleagues who helped organize this successful event! (photo omitted)

Section 3
Announcement and Agenda of an Academic Conference

Warm-up

Suppose you were a researcher in Biology and planned to attend the following conference, what information would you highlight in the following announcement?

Dear Colleagues,

With great pleasure we announce the 13th International Conference on the Critical Assessment of Massive Data Analysis (CAMDA) in Boston, MA, USA, July 11 – 12, 2014, held as official Satellite Meeting to the 22nd Conference on Intelligent Systems for Molecular Biology (ISMB).

CAMDA focuses on innovative methods to analyze massive data sets from life sciences. Over two days, researchers from bioinformatics, computer sciences, statistics, genetics, molecular biology, and other fields present novel approaches to analyze Big Data.

An essential part of CAMDA is its competitive challenge where big heterogeneous data sets are analyzed and outcomes and methods compared. Academic and industrial researchers worldwide are invited to take the CAMDA challenge, to show their expertise in handling Big Data, and to present their results. Submitted abstracts are selected for oral and poster presentations. As in last years, the prestigious CAMDA prize will be awarded for the best presentation. Selected submissions are published in the CAMDA Proceedings as an open access PubMed indexed special issue of Systems Biomedicine.

You can find additional information about the challenge data sets, submissions, etc. at www.camda.info. Some key dates are:
- Abstract submission deadline for oral presentation / 20 May, 2014
- Abstract submission deadline for poster presentation / 25 May, 2014
- Notification of accepted contributions / 30 May, 2014
- Early registration closes / 1 June, 2014

> As in past years, contest presentations are complemented by high profile keynotes (with recent speakers including Sandrine **, Mark **, John **, Terry **, John **, Eran **, Atul **, Nikolaus **, and others). This year, we are delighted to welcome:
> - Chris **, Memorial Sloan Kettering Cancer Center, NY, USA
> - Temple **, Boston University, MA, USA
> - Jun **, Beijing Genomics Institute (BGI), Shenzhen, China
>
> We look forward to seeing you in Boston!
>
> The organizers and chairs of CAMDA 2014
> Chairs:
> Djork-Arné **, Johannes Kepler University, Austria
> Joaquin **, CIPF, Spain
> Sepp **, Johannes Kepler University, Austria
> David **, Boku University, Austria
> Simon **, Marshfield Clinic, USA

For a forthcoming international academic conference, the potential participants need to keep an eye on the announcements or notices published by the conference organization committee to make necessary preparations. Conference announcements and agendas are very important documents for potential conference participants, which give details of a conference, such as the time, venue, program and timetable. Hence, potential participants should read carefully the conference announcements and agendas.

1. Conference Announcement

An academic conference announcement is a formal notice published by the conference organization committee, informing conference participants of conference details. Traditional conference announcements are printed and posted to relevant colleges or institutes, or published on newspapers or professional journals. Now, blessed by technical progress, the conference announcement can reach every corner of the earth within one second via email or webpage.

An academic conference announcement aims to clarify the following aspects of the conference to the potential participants: *what*, *why*, *who*, *when*, *where* and *how*, that is, what the name and the topic(s) of the conference are, why the conference is held, who will sponsor, organize or attend the conference, when and where the conference will be held and how a researcher or a postgraduate gets access to the conference.

(1) **Structure, Format and Content**

The conference announcement is a formal notice. It is to inform the conference participants of the conference activities in detail. Structurally it consists of three parts: Title, Body and Signature. The title, or the name of the conference, is usually put in the middle of the very first line. The body part lies in the middle of the text and provides the primary information of the conference, including the conference topics, the purpose, the time and venue, and access to the conference. The seal or signature of the organizing committee or the chairperson, the contact email box and conference website are put at the end.

Sample 1

13th Conference on Man-Machine-Environment System Engineering

The 13th Conference on Man-Machine-Environment System Engineering will take place in Yantai, China, October 2013. The Conference Sponsor is the Man-Machine-Environment System Engineering Committee of China. The co-sponsor is Scientific Research Publishing (SCIRP), USA. (Please see the web www.mmese.com)

CONFERENCE THEMES

The Conference is designed to bring participants up to date on the MMESE theory and applications.

Since MMESE involves seven relations (see the right figure), the Conference will cover the following topics, but not limit to:

(1) Research on Man Character (M)

(2) Research on Machine Character (M)

(3) Research on Environment Character (E)

(4) Research on Man-Machine Relationship (MMR)

(5) Research on Man-Environment Relationship (MER)

(6) Research on Machine-Environment Relationship (MER)

(7) Research on Overall Performance of Man-Machine-Environment System (MMES)

(8) Applications Research of MMESE

SUBMISSION INSTRUCTIONS

A. Style for Paper

Papers written in English or Chinese will be considered. Papers are generally no more than 4 pages in length (including Figures and Tables). Papers should be written in double-column format.

B. Preparation for Paper

The paper should contain the following information:

a. Article title/subtitle

b. Name of each author (first initials followed by last name) and the author's primary institution, city, and country

c. Abstract of no more than 150 words

d. Several keywords for indexing purposes (exclude words that already appear in the title/subtitle)

e. Text

(a) Level 1 text headings should appear in solid caps, centered; Level 2 headings are lowercase bold caps, flush to the left margin. Level 3 headings are in italics, flush to the left margin.

(b) In the text, each figure (photos, graphs and line drawings) should be high resolution. Do not use shading as background or to indicate differences in quantity (e.g. as sometimes appears in bar graphs); instead, use patterns such as horizontal, vertical, diagonal, and zigzag lines. Line weight should be at least 1 point. Do not use color figures.

(c) Magnitudes of all measured quantities must be given in the International System of Units.

f. References should appear in a separate section at the end of the paper, with items referred to by numerals in square brackets. References must be complete:

(a) Style for papers: Author (first initials followed by last name), title in quotations, periodical, volume, initial and final page number, month, year.

(b) Style for books: Author, title, location, publisher, year, chapter, initial and final page number.

C. Submission for Paper

For safety, all submissions for paper should simultaneously send by email to the following address: mmese@sina.com. A receipt will be sent to the author by email.

Important Note: All notifications and correspondence concerning your submission are sent to you by email. If your email address changes, be sure to notify the Conference.

PUBLICATIONS

The Conference Proceedings will be published by Scientific Research Publishing (SCIRP), USA. The Proceedings will be sent to the ISTP.

IMPORTANT DATES:

Paper submission: February 28, 2013

Notification of acceptance: March 30, 2013

Modified paper submission: April 30, 2013

Notification of conference: August 30, 2013

> Organizing Committee of CMMESE 2013
> - Contact: mmese@sina.com - Conference website: http://www.mmese.info

Please read Sample 1 carefully, and identify the three parts: Title, Body and Signature in the sample.

The conference announcement aims to inform potential participants of the conference details. The information in the announcement relates to "5w's and 1h" (*what*, *why*, *who*, *when*, *where* and *how*), namely the following 6 aspects:

➢ What is the name/title of the conference? What are the topics to be discussed?
➢ Why is the conference held?
➢ Who are the sponsor and the organizer of the conference? Who will be the potential participants of the conference?
➢ When and where will the conference be held?
➢ How does a researcher or a postgraduate get access to the conference?

The name or title of an academic conference consists of two or three parts: type of meeting, related field/area and sequential number. "Conference", "symposium", "colloquium", "seminar" or "workshop" are often used to indicate the type or the scale of a meeting. Then, prepositional phrases with "on" are often followed to indicate the specific field or topics of the conference. Some well-reputed conferences have a long history and have been held regularly at an interval of two or several years, so the sequential number is often put at the very beginning of the conference title, e.g "1st International Conference on Information Computing and Application", "4th International Conference on Mechanics of Advanced Materials and Structures", "8th International Symposium on Teaching English at Tertiary Level", etc.

Topics to be discussed in an academic conference are leading issues or hot issues of the field, which are listed conspicuously to draw the attention of potential participants. Examples are "Fluid-Solid Interaction", "Atomic Force Microscopy", "Research on Machine-Environment Relationship" and "Applied Corpus Linguistics". In the topics technical terms are given in the form of noun phrases rather than long complicated clauses. The listed conference topics communicate the conference focuses to the readers. Accordingly, researchers who deal with the related topics or areas will pay continuous attention to the conference while those whose research issues are not closely related will pass it over. However, driven by the concept of innovation, conferences do not tightly confine the conference topics, but describe the conference topics in a relatively open way, with expressions like "with a particular focus on but is not limited to the following topics" to invite more potential participants to join in.

The purpose or significance of an international academic conference is covered in the conference announcement. This part includes the introduction of the conference history, the impact of the related research on scientific progress and human welfare, and contributions of previous conferences if any. Expressions or sentence patterns such as "was initiated in", "has been held regularly every 2 years", "the most prestigious conference in the field", "approach technological frontier issues", "explore the interdisciplinary development trend", "promote the dissemination of", "provide a forum for researchers and practitioners to exchange research results and share research experiences", "aim to introduce the latest technical development and academic research hot issues, provide a platform for leading researchers to present their state-of-art accomplishment, discuss and share their experiences, and foresee future directions in the field of …" and "is an important platform of academic exchange and aims to keep up with the development trend of applied linguistics and track hot points of linguistic research, highlight groundbreaking progress in …" are often used. Though not stated evidently in some conference announcements, the significance of academic conferences are obvious to all research workers. So, most potential participants will browse this part quickly, and pay more attention to information on the conference time, venue, etc.

Two types of people, conference staff and conference participants make up the majority of an academic conference. The conference staff are very important to a conference due to their great efforts to initiate, organize and run the conference smoothly. The conference staff consist of the sponsor(s), the organizer(s), the organizing committee, the academic committee, the secretariat, etc. The conference participants are mainly researchers of different levels, and among whom are some well-known scientists, scholars and professors.

The time and place of a conference is important information for the potential participants since they can work out the schedule in advance according to the approximate time span and the distance. The conference announcement tends to describe the conference time and place with expressions like "will take place on September 1st, 2005 in Xiamen, China", "will be held in …", etc. In addition to the starting time and meeting place, other important dates are also highlighted to give a clear picture of the submission and the registration process, e.g. paper submission due, paper acceptance notification, minor revision due, final decision due, final manuscript due, camera-ready paper submission due and registration open date.

As regards how to get access to the conference, or exactly, how to submit qualified papers, the conference announcement provides a guideline for the paper submitters, which mainly covers requirements in 3 aspects—paper content, paper layout, submission means and deadline. In terms of content the submitted paper should focus on the listed conference topics and be innovative rather than plagiarized. The layout directions stipulate the requirements in the font type, font size, paragraph spacing, the citation style, the tagging format, the image format, the image resolution, etc. Since many factors need to be taken into consideration in the paper layout and different conferences have even different criteria on the layout, a sample of layout is often provided for the submitters' convenience. Besides, the length of the paper and the language written is also stipulated. Finally, the completed paper should be submitted to the given email box or website before the due date. The following examples are adapted guidelines for paper submission in different academic conferences:

"This conference invites submissions of high-quality original research papers exploring the architecture and techniques in integrated terrestrial-satellite networks. Potential topics of interest include, but are not limited to areas listed above."

"Papers should be submitted in two separate .doc files (preferred) or .pdf files: (1) Main Document (including paper title, abstract, key words, and full text); (2) Title Page (including paper title, author affiliation, acknowledgement and any other information related with the authors' identification) through the Manuscript Central. Please register or log in at http://cn03.manuscriptcentral.com/chinacomm, then go to the author center and follow the instructions there."

"Each submission must be accompanied by the following information: (1) an abstract of about 150 words; (2) 3 – 8 keywords; (3) original photographs with high-resolution (300 dpi or greater); (4) eps. or tif. format is preferred; (5) sequentially numbered references; (6) the basic reference format is: author name, 'article name', issue name (italic), vol., no., page, month, year. For example: Y. M. Huang, 'pervateture in wireless heterogeneous …', *IEEE Journal on Selected Areas*, vol. 27, No. 5, pp. 34 – 50, May, 2014; (7) brief biographies of authors (50 – 75 words) and contact information, including email and mailing addresses."

"Each submission will normally be approximately 8,000 words, with no more than 20 mathematical formulas, accomplished by up to 10 figures and/or tables."

Sample 2

Call for papers

2nd International Symposium on Marine Engineering Geology (ISMEG 2019)

Bulletin No.1
First Announcement

Dalian, China
18-22 October 2019

Hosted by
- IAEG Commission 34
- State Key Laboratory of Coastal and Offshore Engineering (SLCOE), Dalian University of Technology

Cooperating Organizations:
- National Natural Science Foundation of China
- Ocean University of China
- Zhejiang University
- Tsinghua University
- Tongji University
- Tianjin University
- Hohai University
- The First Institute of Oceanography, SOA
- Guangzhou Marine Geological Survey
- China National Offshore Oil Corporation
- The University of Western Australia
- Norwegian Geotechnical Institute

The ocean is the cradle of life, and rich in natural resources. With the worldwide boom in exploration and application of ocean resources, a dramatically increasing amount of coastal engineering and offshore engineering facilities have been designed and constructed in recent decades. The rapid development of human economic activities and global climate change have been leading to a big impact on the marine environment, resulting in frequent geological disasters. Under this circumstance, there is an urgent need to have a platform on which the scientists and engineers can show and share their state-of-art research in science and technology in the field of Marine Engineering Geology. The 2nd International Symposium of Marine Engineering Geology (ISMEG 2019) will be held in Dalian, China between 18 and 20 October 2019. The theme of this symposium is "Exploration of Marine Resources and Marine Engineering Geology". It will provide opportunities for scientists and engineers worldwide to discuss recent advances, to share their knowledge and to identify future research directions in the filed of Marine Engineering Geology.

Welcome to Dalian in 2019!

Topics
- Engineering Properties of Marine Soils
- Marine Geological Hazards and Preventions
- Exploration Technique for Marine Engineering Geology
- Hydrodynamics and Environmental Interaction
- Marine Structure Monitoring and Responses to Geological Disasters
- Marine Sediments and Exploration of Gas Hydrate
- Big-data Analyses and Numerical Modelling

Program

Technical session will run over two days consisting of plenary and keynote speeches, delegate oral and poster presentations. Coffee breaks and luncheons will be provided as well as a welcome reception, banquet and tours.

Call for abstracts

Abstracts should be submitted to email address: ismeg2019@sina.com.
Those excellent papers will be collected and considered to be published as a fully refereed special issue of *Engineering Geology* or *Bulletin of Engineering Geology and the Environment*.

Important dates
- Abstract submission Deadline: April, 2019
- Notification of Abstract Acceptance: May, 2019

Please read Sample 2 carefully, and then interpret the conference announcement from the perspectives of what, why, who, when, where and how. To be exact, they are: What is the name of the conference? Why is it held? Who are concerned with the conference? When and where is the conference held? How does a researcher or postgraduate get access to the conference? Besides these, is there anything else that you can draw from the announcement?

Sample 3

9th International Conference on Ubiquitous Computing and Ambient Intelligence (UCAmI 2015)
7th International Work-conference on Ambient Assisted Living (IWAAL 2015)
1st International Conference on Ambient Intelligence for Health (AmIHEALTH 2015)

Puerto Varas, Patagonia, Chile
December 1-4, 2015
http://mami.uclm.es/ucami-iwaal-amihealth-2015

The conference proceedings in the Springer LNCS series.
Extended versions of selected papers will be published in ISI Journals special issues.

Important dates:
Paper submission: **June 15th, 2015** (extended)
Notification of acceptance: August 15th, 2015
Camera-ready version: September 15th, 2015
Conference dates: December 1-4, 2015

Selected papers will be published in the following journals:
- Journal of Biomedical Informatics
- Sensors Journal
- Journal of Medical Systems
- Health Informatics Journal
(More Journals to be announced)

Impact Factor (2013)
2.482
2.048
1.372
0.787

Conference background & goals:

The Ubiquitous Computing (UC) idea envisioned by Weiser in 1991, has recently evolved to a more general paradigm known as Ambient Intelligence (AmI) that represents a new generation of user-centred computing environments and systems. These solutions aim to find new ways to obtain a better integration of the information technology in everyday life devices and activities.

Several autonomous computational devices of modern life ranging from consumer electronics to mobile phones integrate AmI environments. Ideally, people in an AmI environment will not notice these devices, but they will benefit from the services these solutions provide them. Such devices are aware of the people present in those environments by reacting to their gestures, actions and context. Recently the interest in AmI environments has grown considerably due to new challenges posed by society, demanding highly innovative services, such as vehicular ad hoc networks (VANET), Ambient Assisted Living (AAL), e-Health, Internet of Things, Home Automation and Smart Cities, among others. The main focus of this edition of the UCAmI Conference will be *"Ambient Intelligence: Sensing, Processing and Using Environmental Information"*.

Ambient Assisted Living (AAL) proposes solutions based on Information and Communication Technologies (ICT) to enhance the quality of life of elderly people. AAL promotes the provision of infrastructures and services for the independent or more autonomous living, via the seamless integration of info-communication technologies within homes and residences, thus increasing their quality of life and autonomy and reducing the need for being institutionalized or aiding it when it happens. This edition of IWAAL Conference focuses on *"Development and testing of ICT-based solutions in real life situations which enable and support sustainable care models for older adults"*.

One natural and critical human need, where Ambient Intelligence can be used, is healthcare. In such a domain, ubiquitous systems can be used to improve quality of life of the people. While Ambient Intelligence in health applications is increasingly getting research momentum, it has not reached a level of maturity yet. Reasons for such deficiency include not only the challenges of understanding the health domain by computer scientists, but also the difficulty of dealing with such a critical domain, where errors are unacceptable. This first edition of the AmIHEALTH is aimed at boosting this area of research by focusing not just on innovations on the infrastructure and technology required for achieving the ambient intelligence in health, such as smart environments and wearable medical devices, but also on the development of novel testing, verification and evaluation techniques that make possible the actual implementation of such innovations.

UCAmI Topics	IWAAL Topics:	AmIHealth Topics:
Ad Hoc and Sensor Networks: - Middleware for wireless sensor networks - Networked sensing and control - Sensor fusion, tracking and positioning - Embedded software for sensor networks - Environmental sensing applications - Body sensor networks - Vehicular ad-Hoc networks - Network protocols for smart environments **Human Interaction in Ambient Intelligence** - Human-centric interfaces for AmI environments (multi-modal, touch computing, NFC, 2D codes) - Context- and location-aware frameworks and Sensing. - Virtual and augmented reality. - Smart-object based interaction, persuasive computing and tangible interfaces. - Ubiquitous and ambient displays. - Detection and support for collaboration, user intentions and activity recognition, analysis of psychological user states. - Digital TV-based interfaces. **ICT instrumentation and Middleware support for Smart Environments and Objects** - Mobile ad hoc networks and Wireless Sensor Networks (WSNs). - RFID and 2-D codes for real-world labelling. - Smart sensors and wearable computing. - Custom made Internet-connected objects. - Semantic middleware infrastructure (Semantic Web, OSGi, DPWS, home automation standards). - Mining techniques to mobile and sensor data. - Contextualized analysis of social and information networks. **Adding intelligence for Environment Adaptation** - Knowledge representation and management for user and environment modelling and understanding (Ontologies, semantic Web, logic, expert systems multi-agents). - Autonomic computing, responsive and proactive systems and dynamic reconfiguration. - Ontologies for user and environment modelling and understanding. - Learning, reasoning and adaptation techniques over context models. - Collaborative smart objects. - Open data applied to smart environments. **Key application domains for Ambient Intelligence** - Social robotics. - Intelligent transport systems (ITS). - Context-aware apps based on Open and Crowd sourced data.	**AAL Solutions:** - AAL solutions to reconcile increase demand with limited resources. - AAL solutions for supporting formal and informal carers. - AAL solutions for prevention and self-management. - AAL solutions to support the shift towards better care at home and in the community. - AAL solutions to facilitate personalised and effective health interventions. **Technological perspective:** - Big data - Internet of things - Smart cities - Urban Analytics - Wearable technologies - Sensor networks - Multimodal interfaces - Health monitoring - Mobile computing - Context and behaviour awareness - Knowledge management. **Human perspective:** - Dependence - Chronic diseases - Quality of life - Active ageing - Social integration - Self-care - Entertainment. - Behavior Change - Training/ Educating Careers. **Business perspective:** - Standards and interoperability - Potential AAL markets - Exploitation strategies - Real experiences - Business-Academia Synergies. **Security and Privacy Issues in AAL** - Security, privacy and trustworthiness in AAL communications and smart environments. - Freedom and privacy in AAL. **Key application domains for Ambient Assisted Living** **Other related topics** - Platforms for the delivery of AAL - Ambient Intelligence for AAL - Context-Awareness in Assistive Environments - Persuasive Computing - Activity modelling and recognition - Behaviour Analysis - Middleware Architectures for AAL - Interoperability and standards - Security and data management - Sensing and Monitoring solutions within AAL	**Infrastructure of AmIHealth Environments.** - Modelling and simulation of smart environments for Health services. - Novel networks architectures suitable for AmIHealth environments. - Body-worn and Environmental sensor networks architectures. **Technologies** for implementing AmIHealth Environments. - Vital Signs Sensors Communications (*ECG, EMG, Blood Oxygen, Blood Pressure, etc...*). - Individual Daily Sensors (*Accelerometer, Microphone, Gyroscope, Camera, Locations, etc*). - Robotics and agent integration in AmIHealth environments. - Virtual reality and augmented reality paradigms used in AmIHealth environments. - Cloud computing and innovative data models in support of e-Health services. - Big data analytics in AmIHealth environments' context. - mHealth **Frameworks** related with AmIHealth environments. - m-Health related frameworks. - Ubiquitous and pervasive e-Health frameworks. **Applied Algorithms** in e-Health systems - Machine learning, pattern recognition, prediction, inference algorithms. - Clinical decision support systems. - Scheduling, resource planning and optimization algorithms. - Health data visualization. - Biosignal processing. **Interactions** within the AmIHealth environments - Clinical user interfaces. - Health usability - Collaborative medicine systems. - e-Learning tools and AmIHealth environments focused on healthcare education. - Affective computing in AmIHealth environments - Cognitive informatics in healthcare. - Awareness technics for AmIHealth environments - sHealth (Smart Cities Interactions) **Applications and Case Studies** of AmIHealth environments - Individual perspective evaluation: (formal/ informal) caregiver, patient or disabled person. - Hospital perspective evaluation: hospital management, nursing care protocols, pharmacy management, clinical information systems. - Business models for AmIHealth environments - Public Health **Metrics** (protocols, procedures and techniques) for Health environments. - Evaluation, Verifications and Reliability - Quality of Service and Energy Efficiency - Security and Privacy **Other Related Topics** - Collaborative medicine systems - New tools in Healthcare education - e-Learning environments for health - Electronic prescriptions - IoT for healt

UCAmI PC Chairs: - Giancarlo Fortino, Università della Calabria, Italy. - Juan Manuel García-Chamizo, University of Alicante, Spain.	**IWAAL PC Chairs:** - Luis A. Guerrero, University of Costa Rica, Costa Rica. - Ian Cleland, University of Ulster, Ireland.	**AmiHealth PC Chairs:** - Ramón Hervás, Castilla-La Mancha University, Spain - Vladimir Villarreal, Technological University of Panama

Types of Submission:

Long papers. *Intend to allow presentation of academic research results of high quality. Submissions must contain an original contribution, and may not have already been published in another forum, nor be subject to review for other conferences or publications. Contributions should include unpublished results of research, case studies or experiences that provide new evidence about the research or application regarding to the main topics. Articles accepted in this category will be published in the proceedings of the event.* ***Long papers must not exceed 12 pages (including figures and appendices).***

Short papers. *Intend to allow presentation of ongoing studies with partial (but significant) results. Submissions must contain an original contribution, and may not have already been published in another forum, nor be subject to review for other conferences or publications. Articles accepted in this category will be published in the proceedings of the event.* ***Short papers must not exceed 6 pages (including figures and appendices).***

Doctoral Consortium. *PhD students are invited to present the topic and progress of their research, in order to obtain feedback from a panel of experts.* ***Papers for doctoral consortium must not exceed 8 pages (including figures and appendices).***

Posters. *Posters will be peer-reviewed by members of the Posters Committee based on originality, significance, quality, and clarity. Poster authors are not required to transfer copyright. Accepted poster papers will be allocated 2 pages in the conference proceedings. In addition to the* ***3-pages submission****, accepted poster authors will be asked to generate a poster and possible demonstration to be displayed in a dedicated poster area and presented during a poster session at the conference (see call for posters).*

Papers format:

Lecture Notes in Computer Science (LNCS). Please ensure that your papers are formatted correctly and are within the specified page limits. Author information and templates are available in Information for LNCS Authors web*, or download the templates here for* Latex *and* Word*. All papers should be written in English.*

Submission Procedure:

All paper types must be submitted through the EasyChair system: https://easychair.org/conferences/?conf=ucami-iwaal-amihealth-2015

Conference Venue:

Dreams Hotel (5*), Puerto Varas, Patagonia, Chile
http://www.mundodreams.com/hotel/hotel-dreams-los-volcanes/

> *Please read Sample 3 carefully, and interpret the conference announcement from the perspectives of what, why, who, when, where and how. Is there anything different between Sample 2 and Sample 3?*

Currently, most conference announcements are published on the conference webpage. Without space limit, the online conference announcements are given in more detail than typed conference announcements. Different from traditional brief style, online conference announcements consist of a lot of sub-headings super linked with details of various conference activities, which provide potential participants a more convenient approach to conference-related information. The following example shows downloaded webpages of ICRC-CORDEX 2019.

Sample 4

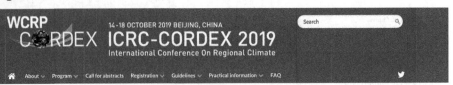

Conference Timeline

22 July, 2018:	First conference announcement released
2 December, 2018:	Call for D-session proposals launched
16 January, 2019:	Session framework launched
February, 2019:	Full conference website launched
20 March, 2019:	Abstract submission launched
	Financial support application launched
	Registration opens
	D-sessions finalized and launched
17 May, 2019:	Financial support application deadline
30 May, 2019:	Abstract submission deadline
5 July, 2019:	Decision on the recipients of financial support—postponed
	Decision on acceptance of abstracts—postponed
15 August, 2019:	Closing of Early Bird Registration
15 September, 2019:	Refund deadline
	Student registration deadline
1 October, 2019:	Closing of Regular Registration
14–18 October, 2019:	ICRC-CORDEX 2019

Venue

China National Convention Center (CNCC)
No.7 Tianchen East Road
Chaoyang District
Beijing 100105, China

Tel: +86 10 8437 3300
Regsitration: Gate C4
Auditorium: 3rd and 4th Floor—F3 and F4
Poster area and parallel sessions: 4th floor—F4

For information on how to get to the China National Convention Center (CNCC), ***click*** here.

Sitting in the center of the Olympic commercial circle between Beijing's fourth and fifth ring roads, the China National Convention Center (CNCC) is only 30 minutes drive to/from the airport and the subway station is connected with CNCC's basement which enables people to quickly go to the city center, the airport, the Beijing Railway Station, and many tourist attractions such as Tian'anmen Square, the Forbidden City or the Summer Palace. It takes only one hour from CNCC to the renowned the Great Wall and the Ming Tombs.

For maps, please ***click*** here.

Call for Abstracts

The abstract submission system is now open. *Click* here.

Before submitting your abstract, please see the General Instructions and register to get your ID to ICRC-CORDEX2019. The payment is not required to submit the abstract.

Requirements

Please note that any submission should be original, and have not been published previous to this submission. Any submission must not violate export restrictions.

Submission of an abstract implies that CORDEX has permission to reproduce the abstract in the program and reports related to the Conference.

Authors are invited to submit an abstract in ENGLISH related to one of the sessions of the symposium.

Note that the abstract should not be more than 2,000 characters including spaces between words.

Maximum file size for uploaded abstracts/files is 30 MB.

A maximum of 3 abstracts can be submitted as first author.

Please register online before submitting your abstract.

Abstracts must be submitted online.

As the number of abstracts that can be accepted for oral presentations is very limited, most accepted abstracts will be as poster presentations.

All submitted abstracts will be evaluated carefully by reviewers. The process means that each abstract will be reviewed within three categories:
▲ Scientific quality: Is the research sound original? Is it well written?
▲ Scientific relevance: Does it fit in the conference session? Does it address the CORDEX themes?
▲ Scientific impact: Does the study have an immediate significant impact in the field? Does it address the large community?

Timeline

Abstract submission launched: 20 March, 2019
Abstract submission deadline: 30 May, 2019, extended
Decision on acceptance of abstract: 10 July, 2019, Postponed

Registration & Conference Terms and Conditions
- **Registration**

The registration is now open. *Click* here.

	On or before 15 August, 2019	After 15 August, 2019	Onsite
Regular	2,600 CNY	3,000 CNY	3,500 CNY
Students & Early Career Scientists*	1,500 CNY		1,500 CNY

* Within 5 years of PhD. Students and Early Career Scientists must supply a letter from their University or Faculty stating current enrolment.

Included in the registration fees: Regular and Student registration fees cover admission to all oral (plenary and parallel sessions) and poster sessions, coffee breaks, conference lunches, as well as a welcome reception on Tuesday 15th October.

Not included in the registration fees: Travel expenses, dinners, per diem or accommodation.

Please note that the deadline for Students / Early Career Scientists registration is extended to 1st October.

Payment can be made using credit card and bank transfer.

Participation is not guaranteed until full payment of the registration fee is received. A personal badge will provide access to the scientific sessions and social events you have registered for.

- **Conference Terms & Conditions**

General

Early registration must be accompanied by payment before the Early Bird deadline (15 August 2019). Otherwise, it will not be processed and the standard registration rates will be applied.

Registrations are for the persons specified and are non-transferable.

Registration for the conference implies the acceptance of the rules of conduct.

Changes to the registration rate selected in the finalized registration form, including received invoice, are only possible for unpaid invoices. In this case, the attendee is asked to cancel the registration order and to place a new one through the registration form, including the correct registration rate. Please note that the deadline for early registration also applies in these cases.

Cancellation Policy

Refund of the registrations fee is accepted with 2,000 CNY (students 1,200 CNY) if notified to icrc-cordex2019@lasg.iap.ac.cn at the latest on 15 September.

After 15 September the registration fee is non-refundable.

There is no reason (including but not limited to illness, inability to travel, visa application rejection, travel restrictions, etc.) for registration cancellation that makes the above-mentioned deadline for cancellations inapplicable.

Insurance

The organizers cannot accept liability for personal accident, loss, or damage to private property, which may be incurred as a result of the participation in the ICRC-CORDEX2019. Participants are, therefore, advised to arrange appropriate insurance coverage. This should apply not only to travel but also to cancellation costs.

Disclaimer

By registering, participants acknowledge and consent that during their attendance at the ICRC-CORDEX2019 their image or voice may be recorded via video, photograph, or any other means by an official of the conference. This content may be distributed or published at the discretion of the ICRC-CORDEX2019. If you do not wish to be recorded, you are required to formally advise the ICRC-CORDEX2019 in advance in sending a mail to icrc-cordex2019@ lasg. iap. ac. cn.

The organizing committee will not accept liability for damages of any nature sustained by participants or loss of or damage to their personal property as a result of the conference or related events.

Registration fees do not include insurance of any kind. The conference participants must accept personal responsibility for insurance against travel risk and injury. While the organizers will make every effort to observe best safety practices, the organizers encourage all participants to purchase adequate medical and liability insurance. Participants save and hold harmless the organizers from any and all claims, losses and damages, on account of events beyond their control.

Poster Presentations Guidelines

A poster communication at the ICRC-CORDEX2019 workshop is a great opportunity to support in-depth presentation of your work, results and achievements, and is very efficient for conveying messages to a large audience with time for questions and productive exchange with other participants. Poster sessions are a key component of the conference programme.

The Conference format places high importance on poster presentations. The program will include several poster sessions, covering a broad range of climate change relevant topics, to allow ample discussions in a studious, yet relaxed atmosphere. Poster sessions especially facilitate interaction between students / early career scientists and more senior researchers.

Poster Display

Posters should be on display as outlined in the poster session. Posters should be put up just before the scheduled display time and taken off at the very end of the scheduled display time. Authors should be in attendance during the session and are expected to stand by their poster in order to answer questions.

Presenters will be asked to remove their poster at the end of their poster session. The posters not removed during the appropriate time will be recycled. Please DO NOT LAMINATE your poster unless you plan to re-use it. Un-laminated posters can be recycled.

Poster Format

Maximum poster are 118 cm (height) x 84 cm (width) = A0 in PORTRAIT. Poster areas will be equipped with poster boards and material to hang your poster up.

Poster ID

Posters are identified with nomenclature according to the sessions A1, B2, C3. For example, the following poster ID "A3-P-01" refers to a presentation assigned number 01 in poster session A3.

NOTE: No local poster printing service will be available during the symposium, so please bear in mind to print and bring your poster.

TIPS for Your Poster

The purpose of a poster is to effectively communicate your work to a particular audience. You need your poster to be attention-seeking and convey a clear message that the audience will quickly comprehend.

There are 4 key elements in creating an effective poster:
- Attract interest
- Help your audience navigate the poster
- Give them content worth reading
- Make it easy to comprehend

The presentation must cover the material as cited in the corresponding submitted abstract.

Use the official abstract title as submitted and make it easy to read. Complement the title with a short abstract that conveys your main message and attracts people passing by. Place the title on top of your poster together with the author's names.

Highlight the author's names, emails, and address information in case the viewer is interested in contacting you for more information and/or provide a card or handout with your contact details.

Organize your material into sections; give each section a sentence heading summarizing it.

Create an attractive design with lots of white space.

Use the same artistic style throughout your poster.

Limit details that don't contribute directly to your main message.

Eye movement: The movement (pathway) of the eye over the poster should be natural, down the columns from left to right. Size attracts attention. Arrows, pointing hands, numbers, and letters can help clarify the sequence.

Topography:
- Avoid abbreviations, acronyms, and jargon.
- Use a consistent font throughout.
- Use type size that is readable from 2 m away. Title text should be at least 54 pt, headings at least 36 pt, and body text at least 28 pt. Keep the number of text characters in a line between 30 and 70. Consider the spacing between the lines.
- Blank spaces are not a problem. Use space to highlight and shape the main content. Used effectively, blank spaces can help the audience to navigate the poster.

If several people gather around your poster, they should all be able to read the text simultaneously.

Use graphics as much as possible to get your message across. Prepare all diagrams or charts neatly and legibly.

Simplicity: Resist the temptation to overload the poster. More material may mean less communication.

Poster No Show

Participants are strongly urged to inform the organizers in case of no-show in sending a mail to icrc-cordex2019@lasg.iap.ac.cn with copy to Catherine Michaut

Stylistically, an academic conference announcement is a formal written discourse, which accords with the conference purpose. An international academic conference is an influential event in the specific research area and draws much attention of scholars and researchers from home and abroad. Additionally, the conference announcement is published by formal institutions, such as Ministry of Education, prestigious universities and institutes. In accord with the formal style, the language is formal, which can be detected easily in the text, e. g. the well-designed layout, blocked writings, technical terms, capitalized letters and usage of the 3rd person.

In terms of language features, an academic conference announcement is brief and concise so as to save space on one hand and to highlight important information on the other hand. Noun phrases, rather than lengthy sentences, play a big part in the conference announcement. Serial numbers or sequential markers are often used to serve the purpose.

Refer to Samples 1 – 4 and identify the stylistic markers of conference announcements in the above samples.

(2) **Useful Expressions and Sentence Patterns**

take place / be held	召开
Conference Sponsor	会议发起人
Co-sponsor	合作者
... is hosted/sponsored by State Key Laboratory	……由国家重点实验室主办/赞助
cover the following topics, but is not limited to ...	涵盖但不限于以下话题……
promote the dissemination of ...	促进……的交流
provide a forum for researchers and practitioners	为研究者和从业者提供平台
share research experiences	分享研究体验
track hot points of ...	追踪……的热点
bridge the gap between ... and ...	搭建……和……的沟通桥梁
keep up with the development trend of ...	紧跟……的发展趋势
highlight groundbreaking progress	凸显突破性进展
main document	主文档
full text	正文
title page	标题页
author affiliation	作者信息
author biography	作者简介
acknowledgement	致谢
manuscript central	投稿中心
register / log in	注册
original photographs with high-resolution	分辨率高的原创图片

continued

DPI = dots per inch	每英寸点数（打印机、扫描仪等的清晰度参数）
sequentially numbered references	按顺序编号的参考文献
title in quotations	引文标题
initial and final page number (or pp.)	起至页码
level 1 text headings	一级标题
bold caps, centered	粗体大写，居中
flush to the left margin	左对齐
horizontal, vertical, diagonal, and zigzag lines	横线、竖线、斜线和波浪线
paper submission due / deadline	论文提交截止日期
paper acceptance notification	论文录用通知
minor revision due	论文微调截止日期
final decision due	最终决定截止日期
final manuscript due	最终稿提交截止日期
registration open date	注册开放日期
camera-ready paper submission due	影印版提交截止日期
notifications and correspondence	通知和联络
registration form	注册表

2. Conference Agenda

A conference agenda is a list of conference activities to be held. A successful conference cannot do without a productive conference agenda. The conference agenda and the conference program are different names of the same document. A detailed and carefully made conference agenda acts as a guide to the conference participants, listing a series of activities to be done at a definite time and place and assisting the participants to fulfill their activities in order.

(1) **Format and Content**

A conference agenda usually takes the form of a table and is printed on a sheet of paper or a small booklet. Normally it reaches the conference participants together with the invitation letter 3 to 6 months before the conference opening.

The content of a conference agenda includes:
- ➢ Title of the text
- ➢ Place of the conference
- ➢ Time of the conference
- ➢ Events in time sequence: Event 1, Event 2 ... Event N
- ➢ Speakers/chairpersons/participants in the events

➢ Topic/titles/themes of the events

Samples are as follows:

Conference Agenda
Day One

Time	Program	Speaker	Topic
8:30–9:30	Opening Ceremony Group Photo	Host	
		Speech given by the leader of International Energy Agency	
		Speech given by the chairman of the conference	
9:30–10:30	Host	Prof. John Watson & Prof. Peter Robert	
	Plenary Session 1	Prof. William Smith	Basics of clean energy, renewable energy sources
10:30–11:30	Host	Prof. Bob Thomas	
	Plenary Session 2	Prof. Steven Johnson	Clean solar energy technologies
11:30–13:00	Buffet-style Lunch		Venue: 2nd Floor of Bononcini Canteen
13:00–13:30	Lecture	Bob Jacobson	Dynamic life cycle assessment of renewable energy technologies
13:30–14:00		Mike Black	Social acceptance of renewable energy innovation
14:00–14:30		Watson Kempton	Vehicle-to-grid power implementation: From stabilizing the grid to supporting large-scale renewable energy

Program Schedule, May 23nd, 2014 (Saturday)
Venue: 1st floor of Barnes Hall

International Conference on New Challenges in Organic Synthesis

	November 27, Sunday		
时间 Time	报告人 Speaker	题目 Title	主持 Chair
8:30–8:40		广东工业大学校领导致开幕辞 Opening Ceremony (Leader of Guangdong University of Technology)	张力 副校长 Li Zhang Vice-President
8:40–8:45		大会主席 Keiji Maruoka 致辞 Speech from Keiji Maruoka (Chairman of the Conference)	
8:45–8:50		日本化学学会主席 Hisashi Yamamoto 致辞 Speech from Hisashi Yamamoto (President of the Chemical Society of Japan)	
8:50–9:10		参会嘉宾与领导合影 Photos	
9:10–9:40	Hisashi Yamamoto	Substrate Controlled Chemical Reaction—Future of Organic Synthesis	江焕峰 Huanfeng Jiang
9:40–10:10	涂永强 Yong-Qiang Tu	Total Synthesis of Natural Products via C-C Rearrangement	
10:10–10:40 **Tea Break & Photos**（茶歇、合影）			

(2) Useful Expressions

program, schedule, timetable, agenda	安排,计划	registration	注册
check in	入住(旅馆)	reception	接待
badge	徽章	ceremony	典礼
concurrent	平行的	plenary	全体的
under the auspices of	在……的赞助下	tea/coffee break	茶歇
lunch break	午餐	buffet dinner	自助晚宴
group photo	合影	address	演讲
presentation	陈述	breakout group	分组
session	会议	briefing	简介会/简报
tutorial	辅导课程	symposium	大会
seminar	研讨会	panel	小组
colloquium	研讨会	track	辑/场
satellite meeting	卫星会议	chair	主持人
undertake	承办	moderator	主持人
panelist	小组成员	guided tour	陪同观光
field trip	实地考察	social events	社会活动

Exercises

❶ **Answer the following questions to have a global picture of conference announcements and agendas.**

(1) What are the important documents that potential conference participants should pay attention to?

(2) What are the main parts of a conference announcement?

(3) What are the differences between a conference announcement and a conference agenda?

❷ **The following expressions are often seen in "Call for Papers" announcements. Match the expressions on the left with the explanations on the right.**

(1) symposium   A. a time or date before which a participant should make an official record of a conference or an activity

(2) proceedings   B. written records of presented papers and discussions at a meeting or conference

(3) registration deadline   C. complete paper is expected to be submitted at a time before …

(4) full text due on …   D. a kind of meeting, exclusively for specialized academic discussion

(5) template   E. add something to a list of …

(6) issues and areas   F. a model on which submitted papers should be based

(7) index   G. official notice of allowing a paper to be presented on a conference

(8) acceptance notification   H. topics of discussion

❸ **Translate the following Chinese into English.**

(1) 本会议将促进水资源特征研究及人类社会对水资源开发与利用等相关领域的跨学科交流。

___

(2) 网上注册参会,请先点击本页面上方或下方"注册"键(进入注册页面),然后填写注册表。

___

(3) 请于2008年3月20日前完成并提交随信附上的参会表格和发言人信息表,以便于我们为大会提供正确信息并及时通知大会动态

___

(4) 您所有住宿及相关费用均由大会组委会支付。

___

❹ **Read the following announcement from ICAIS and fill in the blanks with appropriate words. Then interpret the conference announcement from 6 aspects—*what*, *why*, *when*, *where*, *who* and *how*.**

__(1)__ for Papers—ICAIS

The 5th International Conference on Artificial Intelligence and Security (ICAIS 2019), formerly called the International Conference on Cloud Computing and Security (ICCCS), will be __(2)__ on July 26 - 28, 2019 at New York University, New York, USA. The organizing committee is excited to invite you to take part in ICAIS 2019, to discuss issues at the technological frontier of society today as well as interdisciplinary technological trends.

Topics of interest __(3)__, but are not __(4)__ to:
- Artificial Intelligence
- Big Data
- Cloud Computing and Security
- Information Hiding
- IoT Security
- Multimedia Forensics
- Encryption and Cyber Security

Paper Submission

All submissions must be in English. This year we are accepting full paper and short paper submissions. Full papers must be at least 12 LNCS pages in __(5)__ but no more than 15 LNCS pages, including figures and references. Short papers must be 4-7 LNCS pages in length, including figures and references. Authors should refer to the conference submission __(6)__ to prepare their papers.

The submitted papers must not be __(7)__ published anywhere, and must not be submitted to any other conferences before and during the ICAIS 2019 review process. For any accepted paper, at least one author must __(8)__ and attend the conference to present the paper.

Acceptance

Manuscripts should present the current research in areas identified in the call for papers. All submitted manuscripts will be __(9)__ by experts in the field and will be judged on problem significance, contributions, __(10)__, correctness, technical strength, quality of presentation, relevance, and value to conference attendees.

Publication

Outstanding papers will be invited for possible publication in SCI- __(11)__ journals.

All accepted papers will be published in LNCS and other journals.

Important Dates

Paper Submission __(12)__: November 10, 2018
Notification of Acceptance: December 1, 2018
Registration Due: December 17, 2018
Camera-Ready Paper Due: December 31, 2018
Conference Date: July 26-28, 2019

International Conference on Artificial Intelligence and Security
Tel: +86-(25)-58731244   Email: icccsconf@yeah.net

what	
why	
when	
where	
who	
how	

❺ **A seminar was held in Wuhan University of Science and Technology. Read the following conference information in Chinese, and then work out a conference agenda in English.**

跨文化交际研讨会将于 2018 年 6 月 15 日在武汉科技大学召开,该会议为期一天,具体安排如下:

8:00—9:00,参会人员在行政大楼 1 楼大厅接待处报到。

9:00—10:00,在行政大楼 18 楼报告厅举行开幕式,邀请国际交流处处长讲话、会议主席讲话。

10:00—11:00,在行政大楼 18 楼报告厅举行全体大会,邀请 Jack Smith 教授和 Wu Min 教授做主旨发言,讲座主题分别为"跨文化交际研究的现状和趋势"和"汉语的全球化展望"。

11:00—11:30,在报告厅左侧小厅茶歇,随后在行政大楼门前广场集体合影。

11:30—13:00,小组讨论,第一小组在行政大楼 1102 室,讨论主题为"跨文化交际能力的内涵及测评",由 Peter Johnson 教授主持。第二组在行政大楼 1103 室,讨论主题为"对外汉语教学中的问题及挑战",由 Black Andrew 教授主持。

13:00—14:00,在聚怡餐厅 1 楼大厅用餐(自助餐)。

14:00—15:00,在行政大楼 18 楼报告厅举行闭幕式,邀请外国语学院院长讲话、会议主席讲话。

Conference Agenda

Section 4

Channels of Obtaining Conference Information

> As a postgraduate student, you are supposed to take part in academic conferences frequently to learn about the latest research progress and current research focus. Then how do you obtain the conference information? Listed below are some possible channels to obtain conference information. Share with your partners on your own experiences of conference information searching, and list other channels of information obtaining if you know.
> - Consult the tutor or the seniors in the research group
> - Retrieve information online with the research topic as the keyword
> - Check the main professional journals to search for conference announcements
> - Take advantage of the databank of WOS in the e-library, detect related conference papers and then retrieve the source conferences

The previous section discusses how to comprehend information and obtain valuable information. However, a lot of postgraduates have no idea where to obtain conference announcements, or to obtain authentic and valuable conference announcements. Conference announcement retrieval is a challenging and time-consuming task though people nowadays are surrounded with tons of information every day. So, this section will illustrate how to retrieve the related academic conference announcements, namely, channels of obtaining conference information.

1. Specialized Periodicals and Professional Journals

Both specialized periodicals and professional journals are good channels for conference information. Compared with professional journals, specialized periodicals are more specific, focusing on a narrower field and displaying a deeper insight into one specific field. However, they both transmit messages of important academic meetings concerned besides valuable academic papers. On the webpages of those periodicals, or in the book, readers can see conference announcements of some globally well-known academic conferences in the field. The following are two examples: "ICHD' 2018 —The 13th International Conference on Hydrodynamics First Announcement", published in *Journal of Hydrodynamics*, and Preliminary Announcement for the Second International Conference on HSLA Steels, published in *Journal of Materials Science & Technology*.

   Available online at https://link.springer.com
http://www.jhydrod.com/
2018,30(1):178

ICHD' 2018 — The 13th International Conference on Hydrodynamics
First Announcement
September 2-6, 2018 Sheraton Grand Inchecon Hotel Songdo, Incheon Korea

The 13th International Conference on Hydrodynamics (ICHD'2018) will be held in Incheon, Korea on 2-6 September, 2018.

The first International Conference on Hydrodynamics (ICHD) was initiated in 1994 in Wuxi, China. Since then, 12 more ICHD conferences were held in Hong Kong, Seoul, Yokohama, Tainan, Perth, Ischia, Nantes, Shanghai, St Petersburg, Singapore, and Egmond aan Zee. Evidently the ICHD conference has become an important event among academics, researchers, engineers and operators, working in the fields closely related to the science and technology of hydrodynamics. The coming ICHD'2018 conference will be hosted and organized by Seoul National University (SNU).

We invite you to join the 13th International Conference on Hydrodynamics, and all of you will be warmly welcome to Incheon, Korea.

Conference Themes

The conference will cover all issues related to all fields of hydrodynamics, including in ship and ocean engineering, mechanical engineering, and civil engineering. Specific themes include, but are not limited to:

- Theoretical hydrodynamics
- Linear and non-linear waves and current
- Ship and naval hydrodynamics, including resistance, propulsion, power, seakeeping, manoeuvrability, slamming, sloshing, impact, green water, wake flow,...
- Cavitations and cavity flow
- Ocean, coastal engineering
- Fluid-structural interactions and hydroelasticity
- Hydraulic engineering
- Industrial fluid dynamics
- Computational fluid dynamics(CFD)
- Ocean and atmosphere dynamics
- Environmental hydrodynamics
- Advanced experimental techniques

Particularly we Strongly encourage the participation from non-marine engineering fields, which as mechanical, civil, aero and bio fluid engineering

Abstract Submission

Abstract (200-400 words) can be submitted through website or by e-mail to ICHD2018@snu.ac.kr before the due date. The acceptance of abstract will be noticed by E-mail.

Key Dates:

Receipt of abstract	November 30, 2017
Provisional acceptance	January 31, 2018
Receipt of full papers	April 30, 2018
Final acceptance	May 31, 2018
Preliminary programme and early registration	June 30, 2018
Final programme	July 31, 2018
Conference	September 2-6, 2018

Organization:

Conference Chair: Prof. Yonghwan Kim (Department of Naval Architecture & Ocean, Engineering, Seoul National University)
Sponsoring Organizations:
- Lloyd's Register Foundation Center at SUN (LRFC)
- Advanced Marine Engineering Center
- College of Engineering, Seoul National Univeraity

Contants us:

Secretariat of ICHD 2018
Advanced Marine Engineering Center, Seoul National University
E-mail: ICHD2018@snu.ac.kr
Tel: +82-2-880-2599, Fax: +82-2-876-9226
Website: http://mhl.snu.ac.kr/ichd2018 (will be available from July, 2017)

• Conference

Preliminary Announcement for the Second International Conference on HSLA Steels

General Information

The Chinese Society of Metals is pleased to announce that The Second International Conference on HSLA Steels (HSLA '90) will be held in Beijing, China in October,1990. Much progress in research and development of HSLA steels has been achieved by the world's metallurgical and materials community since the previous International Conference HSLA Steels '85 was held in Beijing. The aim of the conference is to review and to consolidate the scientific, metallurgical, and economical results and to assess the future trend of development in the fields.

Co-sponsors of the Conference

ASM International
Associacao Brasileira de Metais
Association Technique de la Siderugie Francaise
Associazione Italiana di Metallurgia
The Indian Institute of Metals
The Institute of Metals, London
The Iron and Steel Institute of Japan
The Japan Institute of Metals
The Minerals, Metals, and Materials Society

International Advisory Board

M. Cohen (Chairman)
Lu Da

Blanchard M.G.;   Chandra T.
DeArdo A.J.;   Golovanenko S.A.
Gray J.M.;   Jonas J.J.
Kalla U.;   Ke Jun (T. Ko)
Korchynsky M.;   Lui Jia He
Pickering F.B.;   Sage A.M.
Shouhua Zhang.;   Stuart H.
Takechi H.;   Tamural I.

Scope

The main theme of the conference is cost-effective and technology-feasible HSLA steels in production and applications. Papers on research and development, industrial production, commercial applications including specifications and fabrications of HSLA steel are welcome. Review articles and historical perspectives that present long-time fatigue and corrosion data are encouraged.

Session topics include:

Alloy design concepts
--B,Zr,RE,Nb,V,Ti in HSLA steels
--Multiple microalloying and compositional optimization

New trends in technology
--steelmaking practices for improved cleanliness control of gas contents; inclusion shape control; continuous casting and solidification
--austenite grain boundary pinning; thermal and mechanical effects
--controlled cooling and heat treatment integrated with hot rolling
--combination of metallic hot dip coating with heat treatment
--lubrication in hot rolling
--welding
--environmental degradation

New trends in equipment
--combination of metallic hot dip coating with heat treatment
--lubrication in hot rolling
--rolling mill design
--cooling of flat product section and bars

Applications, economic and technical analyses
--economic and technical analyses
--designing with HSLA steels
--examples of weight and cost reducing potential of HSLA steels
--welding developments
--environmental degradation

Development of new products
--microalloyed long products: concrete reenforcing bars, wire rods, rails, etc.
--microalloyed strips and plates
--microalloyed cold-rolled sheets

2. Conference Documents

Some academic conferences have a long history and are held regularly at an interval of two years or more. Usually at the end of this-year conference, the general information of the next conference is publicized in the conference brochures, including the time, the date and the themes. The participants can then start preparation for the next conference. Now the brochure is replaced by the conference announcement on the webpage. The following is an example of year-2021 conference announcement, which was published on the webpage at the end of year-2020 conference.

CALL FOR PAPERS – SAC 2021
The 36th ACM Symposium on Applied Computing
March 22 – 26, 2021, Gwangju, Korea
http://www.sigapp.org/sac/sac2021/

SAC 2021:
For the past thirty-five years, the ACM Symposium on Applied Computing (SAC) has been a primary gathering forum for applied computer scientists, computer engineers, software engineers, and application developers from around the world.
ACM SAC is structured in multiple technical tracks. Each track is devoted to a specific research area, and is coordinated by one or more Track Chair(s). The complete list of the technical tracks selected for the current edition of SAC can be found on the SAC 2021 website.
SAC 2021 is sponsored by the ACM Special Interest Group on Applied Computing (SIGAPP), is hosted by Chosun University and by Chonnam National University, Korea, and will be held in the Kimdaejung Convention Center, Gwangju, Korea.

Papers:
Authors are invited to submit original papers in all areas of experimental computing and application development, as covered by the technical programs of the various tracks selected for SAC 2021. Submissions should fall into the following categories:
- Original and unpublished research work
- Reports of innovative computing applications in sciences, engineering, and business areas
- Reports of successful technology transfer to new problem domains
- Reports of industrial experience and demos of new innovative systems

Peer groups with expertise in the tracks focus areas will blindly review submissions. Accepted papers will be published in the symposium proceedings and ACM digital library. Submission guidelines can be found on the SAC 2021 website. Prospective papers should be submitted to the track using the START submission system. Submission of the same paper to multiple tracks is not allowed.
For more information please visit the SAC 2021 website.

Tutorials:
The Tutorials Program is an integral part of SAC 2021. The organizing committee solicits tutorials that tend to stress state-of-the-art technologies directly applied to the practitioners' field. Presenters are invited to submit proposals for tutorials in all areas of experimental computing and application development. Tutorial's duration is either full day or half day. The tutorial proposal should include a brief summary and outline specific goals and objectives, expected background of the audience, and a biographical sketch of the presenter(s). All tutorial proposals should be directed to the Tutorial Chair. Tutorial submission guidelines will be posted on the SAC 2021 Website.

Potential Tracks:
Bioinformatics and Computational Biology; Business Process Management & Modeling; Cloud Computing; Code Analysis and Software Mining; Computational Intelligence and Video & Image Analysis; Computer Security; Cyber-Physical Systems; Databases and Big Data Management; Data Mining; Data Streams; Decentralized Applications with Blockchain; Dependable, Adaptive, and Secure Distributed Systems; Embedded Systems; Evolutionary Computing; Geographical Information Analytics; Health Informatics; Information Access and Retrieval; Intelligent Robotics and Multi-Agent Systems; Internet of Things; Knowledge and Language Processing; Knowledge Discovery and Information Systems; Knowledge Representation and Reasoning; Machine Learning; Mobile Computing; Networking; Operating Systems; Privacy by Design; Programming Languages; Recommender Systems; Requirements Engineering; Semantic Web and Applications; Software and Hardware co-dependability; Software Architecture; Software Engineering; Software-intensive Systems-of-Systems; Social Network and Media Analysis; Software Platforms; Software Verification and Testing; Sustainability of Fog/Edge Computing Systems; Video Processing for Human Behavioral Analysis; Web Technologies; and Wireless Communications and Networking.

Sample Post-Conference Journal Publications
Typically, extended papers of SAC publications are published in selected SCI-indexed journals (usually with Track Chairs as Guest Editors); among others, we can mention:
- Journal of Computer Languages, Systems and Structures, Elsevier
- Science of Computer Programming, Elsevier
- Journal of Innovations in Systems and Software Engineering (ISSE), Springer
- Journal of Intelligent Data Analysis, IOS Press
- Journal of Computer Security, IOS Press
- Journal of Visual Languages and Computing, Elsevier
- Journal of New Generation Computing, Springer
- Journal of Computer Security, IOS Press
- Concurrency and Computation: Practice and Experience, Wiley
- Software: Practice & Experience, Wiley
- Journal of Web Engineering (JWE)
- Software Quality Journal (SQJ), Springer
- Information and Software Technology (JIST), Elsevier

3. Centers/Departments Specialized in Meetings or Other International Communication

Some centers or departments specialize in publishing information of meetings or international communication activities, and researchers should keep an eye on their bulletin boards constantly. For example, China International Conference Center for Science and Technology is an administrative department, and one of its main functions is to publish information on international conferences of science and technology on its webpage. *International Academic Development* is also a core journal co-founded by China National Ministry of Science and Technology and Huazhong University of Science and Technology, publishing the latest conference information in each volume. Researchers and postgraduates can view the webpage and the book regularly to keep up to date with the conferences of their research fields.

4. Learned Societies/Associations/Organizations/Institutions

In learned societies, associations, organizations or institutions, regular meeting circulars are internally made, which announce in advance the professional conferences of various kinds. Hence, research workers can turn to the organizations for conference information. For example, researchers and teachers involved in study of linguistics or language instruction can seek information from associations like National Advisory Committee on Teaching English Language, China Computer Federation, and Chinese Institute of Electronics, which regularly publish related conference information on their webpages.

5. Influential Databases of Academic Resources

In the information era, conference information retrieval is becoming more convenient than before with the use of search engines. Frequently used search engines include www.google.com, www.baidu.com, www.hotbot.com, www.excite.com, www.lycos.com, www.northernlight.com and www.nbci.com.

Besides these general search engines, some specialized search engines are also widely used, such as www.searchconf.net, www.allconferences.com and www.aconf.cn.

As a matter of fact, some influential academic databases are even more friendly and practical than the search engines. For instance, WOS, SCI, SSCI, CPCI and CNKI are all influential academic databases. Included in the academic databases are influential journal articles, conference proceedings, technical reports, books, etc., via which researchers can retrieve related journals and conferences easily. Normally, the above-mentioned academic literature databases are partly or wholly purchased by universities and research institutes and can be accessed by their students and teachers with the distributed account number by their universities and research institutes.

Exercises

❶ Translate the following expressions into Chinese and describe how they assist your research work.

e-library	
information retrieval	
specialized periodicals	
professional journals	

	continued
China International Conference Center for Science and Technology	
International Academic Development	
learned associations	
Springer	
Elsevier	
Wiley	
WOS	
SCI	
SSCI	
EI	
CPCI	
CNKI	

❷ **Fill in the blanks with the words or phrases given in the box to complete the paragraph.**

> technical reports, professional journals, announcements, retrieval, database of academic literature, obtain information, regularly, publish, irrelevant, frequently, conference proceedings, convenient, specialized periodicals, prestigious, journal articles, at the end of

A good master of conference information _____ makes the researchers' work more efficient. There are many ways to _____ in the information age; however, much among them are _____. In academic research work, the following channels are _____ used and proved to be _____. The first source is _____ and _____, which include _____ of influential relevant meetings in the content. The second is conference announcements. Many conferences are _____ in the specific area, with a long history and high authority. Since they are _____ held once every two or three years, they will _____ the conference announcement of the next meeting _____ this meeting. If researchers intend to participate in the next-time conference, they can obtain the information from the webpage of this conference. The third is widely accepted _____, including WOS, SCI, SSCI, EI, CPCI and CNKI. Included in the academic literature databases are influential _____, _____, _____, books, etc., via which researchers can retrieve related journals and conferences easily.

❸ As a postgraduate, you are supposed to participate in related international academic conferences. Where could you obtain the information of related academic conferences? Please list at least three channels to obtain the related information. Students from different disciplines could exchange with each other since many conferences are concerned with interdisciplinary studies.

___

Project

Universitas 21 is a very influential association across the whole world. It aims to promote the development of globally excellent universities and higher education systems. It is also closely related to our course since it organizes various activities regularly to enhance the international academic communication capabilities of postgraduates and interested undergraduates. Please work with your partner, search related information about U21, and then report what you have learned to the whole class, including its goal, its functions and previously-held simultaneous conferences.

International Academic Conference Correspondence

Attending academic conferences involves writing communication. This includes corresponding with conference organizers and paper reviewers at different stages: deciding to attend a conference or not, inquiring conference organizers about conference activities, and communicating with paper reviewers and editors.

Correspondence in the context of international academic conference tends to take the form of email writing. While emails are still primarily an informal mode of communication, the language used in email messages for international academic purposes tends to be formal. This rule also applies to writing letters if conference attendees want to post letters to conference organizers and paper reviewers under some circumstances.

In this chapter, you will get to know how to:
- inquire about conference activities
- confirm or reject attendance
- correspond with paper reviewers or editors

Section 1
Inquiry About Conference Activities

Warm-up

Fill in each blank with an appropriate word from the box.

mandatory	venue	queries
inquire	attendee	format

1. It is _____ that all supervisors attend Friday's meeting.
2. I will _____ when to begin our lessons.
3. The Grand Hotel, _____ of this week's talks, is packed out.
4. I have several _____ about the work you gave me.
5. "All of us together, in that beautiful place," one _____ recalls.
6. The magazine changed its _____ to appeal to a broader constituency.

A planned conference involves a lot of activities. Before attending a conference, we sometimes need to ascertain the details of a conference, from its authenticity to its agenda to the place where to put your luggage. In most cases we write letters or emails to inquire. So, a conference inquiry letter or email is written by a conference attendee who has certain doubts about the conference. And these doubts could be various, from what the conference is going to be about to the time or the venue at which the conference is to be held.

The following is a brief review of the format of a letter and an email.

The format of a letter:

> **Heading** (writer's address)
> **Date**
> **Inside address** (receiver's name and address)
> **Salutation**
> **Body part**
> (the 1st paragraph: purpose of writing the letter)
> (the following paragraphs: more information and details)
> (the last paragraph: restatement of the writing purpose and thanks to the addressee for reading and responding to the letter)
> **Complimentary close**
> **Signature**

The format of an email:

> **To**: (receiver's email address)
> **From**: (sender's email address)
> **Subject/Re**: (the topic or subject of the email)
>
> **Salutation**
> **Body part**
> **Complimentary close**
> **Signature**

An inquiry letter or email has the same format as a regular letter or email has. Then comes the conference inquiry letter, the topic of this section.

A conference inquiry letter tends to be written in a formal and polite manner. Here are some tips for writing of conference inquiry letters:

(1) Write in a formal style
(2) Include essential details
(3) Be specific
(4) Request for extra information if necessary
(5) Use polite words
(6) Leave sufficient time to the addressee to respond and thus do not mention any date for response

Read the following samples to get familiar with the formats and writing style of conference inquiry letters or emails.

Sample 1

To: name@gmail.com

From: name@gmail.com

Subject: Inquiry on conference to be held

Respected Sir,

  I received news from my colleagues about the environment protection conference organized by your association in December and I would like to inquire about the details and requirements to attend the said conference.

  I am a strong advocate of wanting to protect the environment, and hence I have a few questions to ask regarding the conference. Since I am not a member of the organization, will I still be allowed to sit for the conference? If so, am I supposed to pay an extra amount of money or none at all? How should I apply to be a part of the conference?

  I have been an environmentalist for a long time, and I am really interested in attending your activity.

  If you need to contact me, you may reach me at ... (phone number).

Sincerely,
Tom Dalton

Sample 2

To: name@gmail.com

From: name@gmail.com

Subject: Conference Inquiry Letter

Dear Sir,

  As told by my colleagues, I recently got to know about the Global Physics Education Conference that is to be held on your college campus.

  I am writing this letter to make certain queries that I have regarding the conference. Since I am not a part of the college faculty, will I be allowed to attend the conference? If so, will I have to pay a registration fee?

  Aside from that, I would also like to know when the conference will be held and if the seating arrangement is on a first-come-first-serve basis? Will the organization be providing us with lunch?

  I have been interested in the academic activities that you have organized for physics teachers for a long time and I really look forward to attending the conference.

  If you need to contact me, you may reach me at ...(phone number).

  I appreciate your positive action.

Sincerely,
Calvin Brown

Besides the letters/emails of inquiry about the conference details, another type of inquiry letters/emails is also widely used by research workers, which is the letter/email of request for or inquiry of financial support. Conference communication is beneficial and valuable to participants, but the fees and expenses involved should be paid first, which might be a large amount of money to students, including the conference fee, the transportation expenses, the accommodation expenses and incidental expenses.

As a matter of fact, there are some possible sources of applying for financial support, mainly by the conference, international organizations, learned societies and by other foundations. Take the conference as an example. Almost all conferences have channels raising funds for operation, so participants may be provided with an opportunity of applying for certain financial assistance from the conference. The assistance can be offered in different ways, covering all the expenditures for the conference, providing international airfares, reducing or waiving registration fees, as well as discharging additional fees for other conference activities, etc. In addition, many foundations and private bodies are also the channels for financial assistance, e. g. National Science Foundation of China, National Social Science Foundation of China, China National Education Ministry, National Science Foundation of the United States, National Social Science Foundation of the United States, and many universities and colleges.

The following are examples of financial application emails:

Sample 3

To: name@ gmail. com

From: name@ gmail. com

Subject: Conference Inquiry Letter

Dear Dr. ***,

  Thank you for your letter dated Feb. 10, 2020. I'm writing to you about the application for my travel support to attend the conference. Attached file is the certificate that our university provides. Is there anything else required for the application?

  I have been keen on this conference and I really look forward to attending the conference.

  If you need to contact me, you may reach me at …(phone number).

  I appreciate your positive action.

Sincerely,
Bill Washington

Sample 4

To: name@gmail.com

From: name@gmail.com

Subject: Conference Inquiry Letter

Dear Professor Smith,

  I have received an invitation to attend the conference on language and culture, to be held in London in September. But my participation is hindered by some financial reasons. I'm trying to get funding for the attendance from different channels since the deadline of conference registration is approaching. Could you give me some advice as to whom I can contact for possible financial assistance for the attendance?

  Many thanks.

Sincerely,
John Green

Exercises

❶ **Read the samples in this section and discuss with your classmates about how to format a letter or an email.**

_____

_____

❷ **Please translate the following expressions into English.**

(1) 组织委员会

(2) 注册成为该协会会员

(3) 会员申请表

(4) 参会费用/大会注册费用

(5) 提交摘要

(6) 主旨发言人

(7) 会议主题

(8) 拥有会议中心的学术机构

❸ **Complete the following inquiry letter based on the information provided in the brackets.**

Dear Mr. Thompson,

  This letter is regarding a seminar that I am interested in registering for. I had received notification over an email regarding a seminar on "Future of Logistics Management". I was informed that Dr. *** was to _____ (主持本次研讨会).

I had a query regarding this seminar. I want to know about _____（研讨会费用）. Also, _____（请问与会者住哪里）? As I am _____（不是协会会员）, will I _____（我有资格参会吗）? Please inform me about _____（会员申请要求）. I would also like to know about _____（研讨会历时多久）and the other incentives that would be provided along with it.

The information provided would be of great help to me and would also provide an insight into the seminar.

Kindly feel free to contact me or send over the details by email. My email address is XYZ@gmail.com.

Thank you _____（谢谢您的回复）.

Sincerely,

Bill Washington

❹ **Compose an inquiry letter according to the following context.**

Bill LIU，中原声学研究所副处长，数年来一直从事水下成像和超声无损检测的研究，想参加第12届声学成像国际学术会议。请告知摘要、论文等信息的提交截止日期。

❺ **Read Samples 3 and 4 carefully, and then discuss with your partner about financial support. Will you apply for financial support to attend a meeting? And if you will, which sample will you follow to write the application letter, and why?**

Useful expressions and sentence patterns for writing of formal letters and emails

- Respected / Dear Editor (Sir / Madam / Dr. Smith / Mr. Lee / Ms. Jones)
- I am writing in response to ...
- I am writing with regard to ...
- I had received a notification over an email relating to a seminar on ...
- I was informed that Dr. *** was to head this seminar. I had a query regarding ...
- As I am from the ... sector, will I be qualified to be a participant?
- We are writing to request ... / to enquire about ...
- Please inform me about the requirements for ...
- I would also like to know about ...
- The details provided would be of great help to me and would also provide an insight into the seminar.
- Kindly feel free to contact me and send over the details by email. My email address is ...
- Thank you. I look forward to receiving your reply.
- I look forward to your reply.
- I attach ...
- I enclose ...
- Please find enclosed ...
- Yours faithfully (when writing to someone whom you do not know or have not met)
- Yours sincerely (when writing to someone whom you have met before or whom you have known or spoken to over phone or was introduced by some other person)

Section 2
Respondence to Conference Invitations

Warm-up

Fill in each blank with an appropriate word from the box.

| stipulate | privilege | prestigious | engagement |
| allot | designate | overhead projector | assign |

1. I'm pleased that we were able to cover all of the objectives today within the _____ time.
2. I'm going to put a pie chart on the _____ so that everyone can visualize how the number has declined.
3. This _____ that emissions of sulphur dioxide must be cut to 10 million tonnes below 1980 levels by the year 2000.
4. Once the tasks were _____ to the newly-recruited committee members, the meeting then turned its attention to the lawyers.
5. The individual owed a duty to society, and had to respect _____ and those who enjoyed them.
6. One of the most _____ universities in the country is looking for a new president.
7. The report _____ the blame for the accident to inadequate safety regulations.
8. I had to refuse because of a prior _____.

1. Conference Invitation

A conference invitation is often sent as a letter. Conference organizers send an invitation to invite someone to be their guest at a conference. A conference invitation letter usually has a formal, business-like style and may contain the following elements:

```
                                    [letterhead: return address]
                                              [Date of letter]
                                [Recipient's first and last names]
                                         [Company/institute name]
                                       [Street or P. O. box address]
                                            [City, State ZIP code]
Salutation
Body part
Complimentary close
Signature
```

Sample 1 (Invitation)

Dear [recipient's name]:

  As you might be aware, we, *** Association, will be hosting our annual *** Conference again this year. This exciting event will take place during May 15 – 17 at the *** Hotel in ***. Many prominent speakers, along with information-packed workshops, will fill the agenda. I am honored to invite you to attend this conference as my guest.

  Please contact *** at ***@###.com to let us know whether you are able to join us at *** Conference. Also, please feel free to contact me if you need further details on the conference.

  I look forward to seeing you in *** this May.

Best regards,

[Signature]

Sample 2（Invitation）

Dear Professor ***,

  We are inviting you to attend our conference on "The Textile Institute 83th World Conference" during August 14 – 16, 2012.

  The conference is jointly organized by College of Textile, Donghua University. The conference will first be opened in Shanghai, and then move to Nottingham. As co-organizer of the conference, you are cordially invited to attend the Shanghai part of the conference, to be held in this university from 14 to 16 June 2012. You will be provided with subsistence allowance and accommodation for the duration of the conference.

  If you have any enquiries or require any assistance, please do not hesitate to contact our Conference Convener, Mr. *** or our Executive Officer, Mr. *** (Tel:021-######). We look forward to receiving you here.

Yours sincerely,

***

***, Chair

Organizing Committee

Sample 3（Invitation）

Dear Professor ***,

  On behalf of the Ohio State University and the IEEE Computer Society, I would be very pleased to invite you to attend and chair a session of the forthcoming 2004 International Conference on Parallel Data Processing to be held in Bellaire, Michigan, from October 25 to 28, 2004.

  We sincerely hope that you could accept our invitation. As you know, this is the 10th anniversary of the Conference, and we plan to make it a truly international meeting. We have accepted many papers from several foreign countries, including two from China. You are an internationally acclaimed scholar and educator. Your participation will be among the highlights of the Conference.

  If you can come, please let us know as soon as possible, since we have to prepare the final program soon. We are looking forward to your acceptance.

Sincerely yours,

***

Exercises

❶ Text styles accord with text purposes, so invitations vary from context. For instance, invitations to different guests vary in style. Please read Samples 1 – 3 and discuss with your partner about their differences in style.

_____
_____
_____
_____

----

2. Responding to Conference Invitations

(1) **Acceptance of Invitation**

If you are invited to a conference, or you are sent the notice that the paper you submitted to a conference is accepted, you need to respond to the reference organizers to tell them if you will attend or not. The following are principles and possible elements when writing an email to confirm your attendance.

① Be direct in your response and avoid any unnecessary expressions of reluctance or modesty.

② Accept the invitation or confirm your attendance with pleasure.

③ If necessary, confirm the following.
- important details and necessary information like location, time and date
- special equipment or materials if you need
- the background information of the audience, their interests and attitudes
- the possible fee involved if it is appropriate
- travel details and lodgings

④ Express good will.

Sample 4（**Reply to Confirm Attendance**）

Dear ***,

  I acknowledge the receipt of your letter notifying me of the acceptance of my (our) paper submitted to ### Conference and I confirm that I (or one of the co-authors) will attend the conference and present the paper.

  Paper No: 01A34

  Title: ###

  I understand that any papers that have not reached you in the final camera-ready form by the 10th day of July, 2021 will not be included in the Proceedings of the Conference, and I accept this.

Yours sincerely,
***

Sample 5（**Reply to Confirm Attendance**）

Dear Dr. ***,

  I have received your letter dated December 28, 2021, inviting me to attend the First International Conference on Wireless Innovations: New Technologies and Evolving Policies to be held in Birmingham, England on 18–20 July 2022. Thank you for your invitation.

  I am pleased to accept your invitation and will send my paper entitled "A Preliminary Discussion on ###" to the Paper Committee before the required date.

  Thank you once again for your kind invitation and for your effort in making the conference a successful one. I am looking forward to meeting you soon in Birmingham.

Faithfully yours,
***

(2) Declination to Invitation

Sometimes you may decline an invitation or refuse to attend a conference for a certain reason. Then you are supposed to write a letter to address the declination or refusal. Remember to obey the following guidelines when you write the declination letter.

① Start with a positive statement and then state that you will not attend the meeting.

② Explain politely why you cannot fulfill the request.

③ Be concise when explaining your refusal.

④ Suggest an alternative plan if it is necessary or possible.

⑤ Write a positive statement at the end to appreciate the reader's goodwill.

Sample 6 (**Reply to Decline Attendance**)

Dear [Recipient's Name],

I feel sincerely honored and privileged that you have invited me to be the guest speaker at the upcoming international conference of ×××. I am fully aware that this will be a prestigious event, considering that you also invited quite a few famous scholars to this gathering.

Regrettably, as much as I want to attend, I will not be able to do so because I will be on another conference that I have confirmed to attend.

With that, I would like to suggest Ms. ... to take my place as guest speaker. Ms. ... has been invited several times in speaking engagements. She has been in the field of ... for 30 years, and she is an expert in ... I can assure you that she is highly equipped with the latest trend in ... and has an excellent grasp of topics assigned to her. Just let me know if you decide to invite her as my alternate so that I can inform her ahead.

Once again, my sincere thanks to you for your invitation. I wish this conference will be a great success.

            Sincerely,
            [Sender's Name]
            [Sender's Title] -Optional-
            [Enclosures: number] -Optional-
            cc: [Name of copy recipient] -Optional-

Sample 7 (**Reply to Decline Attendance**)

Dear Professor ***,

Many thanks for your letter of October 25, 2005, inviting me to attend and chair a session of the forthcoming Second International Conference on the Knowledge Economy and the Development of Science and Technology to be held in Glasgow, UK, from August 24 to 25, 2005.

Much to my regret, I shall not be able to honor the invitation because I have been suffering from ill health this summer. I am firmly advised that it would be unwise to undertake any distance travel in the near future.

I feel very sorry to miss the opportunity of meeting you and many other colleagues in the field of the knowledge economy.

I wish the conference a complete success.

            Respectfully yours,
            ***

Exercises

❷ Read the following sample letter to confirm conference attendance. Identify what guidelines this letter follows with reference to the list of guidelines on Pages 13 – 14. Underline the part which follow the guideline and specify which guideline it follows. For example, the superior numeral "[1&2]" means that the underlined part "<u>I am extremely honored by the invitation to speak at the 16th Conference</u>" follows both the 1st and the 2nd guidelines mentioned in this section (1. Be direct in your response and avoid any unnecessary expressions of reluctance or modesty. 2. Accept the invitation or confirm your attendance with pleasure.)

Sample Letter

[Sender's Name]
[Address Line]
[State, ZIP Code]
[Letter Date]

[Recipient's Name]
[Address Line]
[State, ZIP Code]
[Subject: Normally bold, summarizes the intention of the letter] -Optional-
Dear [Recipient's Name],

  <u>I am extremely honored by the invitation to speak at the 16th Conference</u>[1&2] on ××× on Saturday, Oct 10, at 9:00 a.m. My topic on that day will be " ××× " and I shall be able to cover it in the stipulated thirty-minute schedule that you have allotted for me. I hope there shall be adequate arrangements like an overhead projector and screen for me to make my presentation. I again thank you for providing me with this opportunity. I hope to be able to meet with many like-minded people during the conference.

                 Sincerely,

                   ***

Exercises

❸ **Complete the following acceptance to an invitation according to the information in the brackets.**

Dear Mr. ***,

  I'm _____ Speaker _____ the 8th International Conference for Environment Protection Education in Rural Areas _____ Monday, April 10 at 10:00 am _____ the Maria Center in Sunlight.

  For what I will be presenting, I _____ (一台投影仪、一个写字白板、一支白板笔、一个领夹式麦克风). Also, since there will be local geography teachers invited to _____ (观摩大会), it would be very nice if you can send the information _____(关于他们的大致教育背景和课堂活动设计) as I will then be able to prepare the appropriate technical material.

  I'm presently arranging my travel schedule and will pencil in my arrival in Sunlight on Sunday, April 9. You will receive my call during the next seven days _____(确认行程) and to arrange reimbursement. I'm looking forward to the conference.

Sincerely,
***

❹ **Please translate the following expressions into English.**
 （1）激光翻页笔
 （2）安装有 Google Map 的 Windows 系统电脑
 （3）（在会议上）做小组发言
 （4）因为新冠限制无法旅行
 （5）通过 Zoom 进行直播陈述
 （6）通过腾讯会议播放录制好了的陈述

❺ **Read the following invitation letter and discuss with your partners about how to respond to this letter.**

1st International Conference on Zoonoses

16-17, October, 2014

Dear Madam/Sir

The Faculty of Veterinary Sciences, Bahauddin Zakariya University, Multan, Pakistan is organizing **1st International Conference on the Zoonoses** from 16-17, October, 2014. The meeting has been planned with the aim to bring together veterinarians, medical practitioners and laboratory scientists around the theme of zoonoses in Pakistan. The conference will attract and influence its audience through a programme of presentations and panel discussions addressing critical aspects of Zoonoses, with particular emphasis on the prevention and control of zoonotic diseases. The conference will feature presentations by well-known authorities with key role in the areas of research relevant to conference title. Efforts will be made to highlight the areas where new approaches need to be developed and reinforced. A copy of brochure containing details of the conference is enclosed for your kind information. We would greatly appreciate if you kindly circulate the conference brochure among postgraduate students, researchers and faculty members in your organization. Please feel free to contact for any assistance.

We are looking forward to welcome the participants from your prestigious institute at this event.

Regards,

Prof. Dr. Masood Akhtar

Conference Secretariat

Faculty Of Veterinary Sciences, Bahauddin Zakariya University, 60000 Multan, Pakistan

veterinary@bzu.edu.pk

0092619239723 Fax. 0092614745445

Section 3
Correspondence with the Editor / the Paper Reviewer

Warm-up

Fill in each blank with an appropriate word from the box.

revise	resubmit	self-contained
supplementary	reference	in progress
login to	receipt	remove

1. If you wish to obtain _____ information, please contact one of our representatives.
2. We have _____ the irrelevant figures from the table.
3. Completed projects must be _____ by 10 March.
4. Each chapter is _____ and can be studied in isolation.
5. The library contains many popular works of _____.
6. I'll prepare a _____ estimate for you.
7. You must _____ the conference system via the website.
8. To view abstracts that are _____ or already submitted, choose the abstract from your list on your home page.
9. After submitting your abstract, a _____ of your submission will be emailed to you within 24 hours.

Submission to a conference includes submissions of abstracts and full texts to a symposium, or workshops for a conference. In most cases, an abstract is to be submitted first, and then if it's accepted, the full text is submitted. But some conferences request for the full-text submission rather than abstract at the first step. Anyway, the author is required to communicate with the organizer and paper reviewers by writing letters or emails in the process of submission and after it.

1. A Cover Letter of Abstract/Full-text Submission

In the era of Internet, submission to a conference is often processed in the online submission system of a conference. However, there are occasions when authors need to submit to a conference by writing a cover letter, a letter or an email that introduces his/her submission to the organizer or editor.

An effective cover letter of abstract/full-text submission often includes:

- the purpose of submitting
- the title of the paper and corresponding author details
- a brief summary of the author's findings: 3 or 4 sentences to summarize the most important findings of your study
- motivation for submitting: a small paragraph regarding the suitability of the author's study for the conference and its target audience
- conflict of interest: whether there are any potential conflicts of interests
- originality and author agreement: a formal statement that the manuscript has not been published and that all the authors have agreed to submit to the conference

Here are two sample cover letters of abstract/full-text submission:

Sample 1

Dear Editor-in-Chief ***,

  We are submitting the manuscript entitled "###" to be considered for publication in the *ABC* as an original research article.

  In this work, we apply graph deep learning techniques in ... and identify ... To be specific, we first define ... and then propose ... to address the classification problem. The experiment result suggests that ... Additionally, compared with other existing models, this model ... As a high-reputed journal, *ABC* has a long-standing interest in research of metrics by data mining and machine learning, so we wish the readership of *ABC* be interested in this study due to its specific and deep research of influence prediction and citation network analysis.

  We declare that none of the work contained in this manuscript is published in any language or currently under consideration at any other journal, and there are no conflicts of interest to declare. All authors have contributed to, read and approved this submitted manuscript in its current form.

  We hope you find our manuscript of interest and look forward to hearing from you soon. Thank you very much.

> Sincerely,
>
> Dr. ***
>
> Professor at School of ###
>
> ### University of ###
>
> Email: ***@gmail.com
>
> Cell Phone: +86 ######

> **Sample 2**
>
> Dear Dr./Ms./Mr. ...,
>
>   It is with great pleasure that I submit for consideration my article "###". This paper is the product of two years' cumulative work with ***, ***, and ***. Attached is an abstract that covers the major conclusions.
>
>   On the whole, our research explored ... This led to the examination of the importance of ... Our ultimate conclusion unpacks the way that ...
>
>   This manuscript is completely original, and no part of it has been published or considered for publication elsewhere. There are no conflicts of interest with regards to this material, potential reviewers, or publications.
>
>   Thank you for your consideration, and I look forward to seeing this work reviewed.
>
> Sincerely,
>
> ***

2. Online Abstract Submission

Nowadays, abstract submission is often conducted online when a conference provides an online submission system. The following is what a submission system may look like.

> **Abstract Submission Form**
>
>   Abstracts should be in English, with a maximum of 250 words. Please use single spacing and Times New Roman, 12-point font. Abstracts of research papers should provide a brief description of research objectives, methodology, theory and summary of results and/or conclusions. Please do not include any charts, bibliographies or footnotes. Abstracts will be reviewed anonymously.
>
> **Presenter name***
>
> [   ]
>
> **Email***
>
> [   ]

Title of your paper*

[   ]

(Maximum of 50 characters)

Summary of your paper*

[   ]

(Summarize your paper in 50 words or less. Note: This summary will appear in the conference program.)

Full Abstract

(Please copy and paste your full abstract here. Maximum size: 250 words.)

Full Abstract

[   ]

File upload supports pdf, doc, docx, txt & rtf formats. If you choose to submit your abstract in file format, please include your name, title, summary and full abstract in the file.

In this case, the conference attendees only need to read the submission guide and fill out the form carefully to submit an abstract without writing cover letters or emails.

3. A Cover Letter of Re-submission

Normally, after the conference reviewers review the submitted abstracts, the authors may receive a notification of preliminary acceptance. This is an invitation to submit a full text for review. The conference will review the submitted full text to determine if the submission is to be accepted for presentation at the conference or not.

Some of the submissions are declined immediately due to technical or language reasons, while others will receive a review report, usually covering pages of comments and revision suggestions. The revision may be frustration when starting out. Receiving criticism and defending a manuscript takes practice. To respond to reviewers' comments on the submitted manuscripts is essential to the next steps of paper presentation and publication. The leading publisher Elsevier recommends a "CALM" approach for researchers when they prepare for their response to reviewer comments. "CALM" stands for "comprehend", "answer", "list" and "mindful" respectively, which means:

(1) Read the reviewers' decision letter carefully and objectively and make sure you understand the concerns of the reviewers.

(2) Respond to the reviewer politely and objectively.

(3) Create a list so as to cover all the reviewers' comments and address each comment separately below.

(4) Be organized when you resubmit your manuscript. This will help the revision process to run smoothly and efficiently.

A qualified re-submission usually contains four things:

(1) Cover letter: Accompany your re-submission with a brief and polite cover letter which includes your manuscript details and a brief statement to note the re-submission followed by a sincere thanks to the editor for the opportunity to improve and resubmit your work.

(2) List of responses: List the reviewers' comments and your response.

(3) Highlighted revision: Highlight your revision in your revised manuscript. Such tool as Microsoft Word's "track changes" feature (or something similar) will illustrate how and where you have revised the manuscript, which is the best evidence that you have taken the reviewers' comments seriously.

(4) Clean version: Make sure to submit a "clean" version of your manuscript that is ready for acceptance and further production or publication.

Here are examples of cover letters to respond to review comments:

Sample 3 (A Cover Letter of Re-submission)

Paper Number: 12B34

Author(s): *** & ***

Paper Title: ABC

Dear editor and reviewers,

　　We greatly appreciate the thorough and thoughtful comments provided on our submitted article. It has taken us a rather long time to complete the final revision. We made sure that each one of the reviewer comments has been addressed carefully and the paper is revised accordingly.

　　As well, we have incorporated more images for better illustration of the concepts and added quite a few new references pertaining to the latest works on spectral geometry processing in the year 2008.

　　Attached below are detailed responses to all the reviewer's comments. The latter are shown in blue and our responses in red.

　　Please let us know if you still have any questions or concerns about the manuscript. We will be happy to address them, now in a timely manner.

Sincerely,

*** & ***

The authors of paper 12B34.

Exercises

❶ **Read Sample 3 and discuss with your partners about the features of the letter/email from the following perspectives.**

Feature	Tone	Style	Purpose
Comment			

As we mentioned previously, a qualified re-submission usually contains four things—a cover letter, a list of responses, a highlighted revision and a clean version. Sample 3 is an example of a cover letter of re-submission. The following example is a list of responses, listing the reviewers' comments and the author's response.

> **Sample 4 (Detailed Responses to the Reviewer's Comments)**
> Notes: a. This is an adapted and abridged cover letter of re-submission.
>   b. The italicized part is the reviewer's comments and revision suggestions.
>   c. The underlined part is the response from the author(s).
>
> Review #1
>
> ===========
>
> Recommendation
>
> ------------------------
>
> *Accept*
>
> Information for the Authors
>
> ------------------------
>
> *Overall I find that this is a very nice survey, and a timely one, because there is no contemporary work that summarizes all the knowledge regarding spectral analysis of meshes and its applications in graphics. I have some minor comments regarding the manuscript and I hope the authors will consider addressing them, even though I recommended "accept" without revisions. Here are my suggestions in chronological order.*
>
> *It would be better to formulate the abstract and the intro in present tense (i.e. "theoretical background is provided" instead of "will be provided").*
>
> >> <u>Thank you. This is done.</u>
>
> *Sections 1 and 2 talk about the Laplacian without defining it. Surely, there are various definitions, as described later in the paper, but still, it would be beneficial to give the reader some flavor or hint before plunging into the historical survey of Section 2. Otherwise,*

a novice reader will get lost quickly—you talk so long about the spectrum of linear operators, but define one for the first time on Page 7. Consider moving Equation (1) and some of its related formalism to the beginning of the exposition.

>> Thank you for your thorough comment. This is done. The definition of the graph Laplacian is inserted into the start of Section 2. Also, a general description of the Laplace operator is provided at the same time. In addition, we have inserted two new figures to provide clear illustration of the spectral approach and spectral embedding early in the paper.

Page 5, top: The text gives a (false) impression that any $n \times n$ matrix M has n real eigenvalues. Add that only certain types of matrices can be diagonalized, like the normal matrices over the field of complex numbers or symmetric matrices over the real numbers.

>> Thanks a lot for your thorough comment. We could not locate the specified text, but suspect that this might be referring to the second paragraph of Section 5. This issue is now rectified.

Page 8, very end: you say "The new operator does exhibit some nice properties. But a common drawback ...". Please elaborate what "nice properties" mean in your context or remove this sentence (it's too vague). Same claim is repeated on Page 9, top (regarding "T": When used in relevant applications, "T exhibits nice properties"—what applications and what properties?)

>> Thank you very much. These issues are both addressed.

Somewhere in Section 6.2 you should mention the recent works by Wardetzky et al, namely:
"Discrete Laplace Operators: No Free Lunch". SGP 2007.
"Discrete Quadratic Curvature Energies", CAGD 24, 2007.

These works have interesting and relevant discussion about the definition of the discrete Laplacian, the mass matrix and the related inner product on surfaces, symmetry, etc.

>> Thank you for your comment. We added the two references and commented on them in Section 6.2.4 and Section 6.5.

Exercises

❷ Please refer to Sample 4 and respond to the following reviewers' comments properly.

Comment 1: "Section 2 is immediately followed by Section 4 (numbering needs correction)."
Scenario 1: *Actually, Section 2 is followed by Section 3 in the submitted paper.*
Respond 1:

Comment 2: "Page 5, Line 24. The new and key term is wrong in its spelling."
Scenario 2: *The other author doing this part was not careful to find the mistake.*
Respond 2:

Comment 3: "Page 8, Line 3. The function of the PNF Mode is not clearly explained."
Scenario 3: *The function of the mode does need more explanation.*
Respond 3:

Comment 4: "Lagrangian of a graph". This is intriguing (I do not know about that), could you elaborate on that?
Scenario 4: *"Lagrangian of a graph" is left un-defined in the paper. And you added its definition in Section 3.*
Respond 4:

Comment 5: "In the context of shape matching, the fact that there exist non-similar shapes which are isospectral, should be mentioned."
Scenario 5: *You did not mention the non-similar shape issue in your submitted paper. And you add a reference to isospectral graphs in Section 5.1.*
Respond 5:

Comment 6: "The MDS section is a bit out of place in the operators section."
Scenario 6: *The MDS section was in Section 7.2, which is not reasonable. You put the section in a new section: Section 7.2.3, and gave it a new title.*
Respond 6:

When replying to the editor and the reviewers' comments, we should firmly follow three rules, which are "answer completely", "answer politely" and "answer with evidence". In the above sample, although the author does not number the reviewer's points, he/she lists the reviewer's comments one by one and gives point-by-point responses. We can also use headings such as "Reviewer 1"—"Comment 1", "Comment 2" and "Reviewer 2"—"Comment 1", "Comment 2". We should address all the comments in a reader-friendly way, i.e. the editor/reviewers could easily follow what we have listed. It is very important that we address each and every issue that the reviewer or journal editor may have raised. Also, "answer with evidence" is very important, which means making our response well-reasoned: If we disagree with a reviewer's comment, we should say so and provide appropriate details and evidence. When necessary, citation of published studies should also be provided which can help to support our argument.

If we receive a huge list of comments, it usually means that the referee is trying very hard to help us improve the paper to get it accepted. Reject statements are usually short, and do not allow us an open door to resubmit. It is quite all right to disagree with referees when replying, but remember to do it in a way that makes the referees feel valued. Pompous or arrogant remarks such as "we totally disagree" or "the referee obviously does not know this field" should be avoided. Instead, words such as "we agree with the referee ... but ..." are preferred.

Exercises

❸ **Please translate the following Chinese expressions into English and the English into Chinese.**

(1) 提交修改过程

(2) 改稿

(3) 改稿及重新提交通知

(4) 审稿人意见

(5) 同行评议

(6) Manuscripts can be returned without review for reasons that include:
- Grammar and style are not of the quality expected in a published article.
- The topic or scope of the work is not within the scope of the journal.
- The presentation of the findings is not directed to the readership of the journal.
- The methods or approaches are judged to be flawed.

❹ Read the following reviewers' decision letter carefully and answer the questions after it.

> Dear Dr. Wang,
>
> Thank you for submitting your work to XYZ.
>
> Before we pass on manuscripts to the editor, who is responsible for the scientific assessment, we perform an initial check against formal technical criteria (structure of submission, adherence to the Guide for Authors and English language usage).
>
> We regret to inform you that your manuscript has failed in the initial formal technical criteria assessment.
>
> (1) Use of English
>
> In its current state, the level of English throughout your manuscript does not meet the journal's required standard. Authors have the responsibility to present papers in good English which can be understood by the journal's readership. If reviewers cannot understand your work as easily as possible, the acceptance possibility of your article will be lowered greatly. We will not consider a revised version of your manuscript, unless it has received a complete re-writing to improve the level of English.
>
> (2) Structure and Completeness
>
> Your manuscript is not in accordance with every aspect listed within the author guidelines. Your manuscript should include, but not be limited to, the comments mentioned below.
>
> - Language
>   * In its current state, the level of English throughout your manuscript does not meet the journal's desired standard. Please check the manuscript and refine the language carefully.
> - Technical
>   * A minimum of two of the keywords is to be chosen from the list of fixed keywords that can be found at the end of the Guide for Authors.
>   * The maximum number of illustrations is strictly limited to five. If the maximum of 5 illustrations is used, then the total number of words must be reduced to 1,600.
>
> (3) Final Word
>
> If you thoroughly revise your manuscript in accordance with what is stated above in (1) and (2), we welcome you to resubmit it. However, we will again check your manuscript for adherence to technical criteria. Passing this is not a guarantee that your submission will subsequently proceed to the peer review process, which is a decision to be made at the sole discretion of the editor.
>
> Yours sincerely,
>
> ***

1. The major concerns of the reviewers are: _____ .
2. What do the following sentences mean?
(1) However, we will again check your manuscript for adherence to technical criteria.
(2) Passing this is not a guarantee that your submission will subsequently proceed to the peer review process, which is a decision to be made at the sole discretion of the Editor.

❺ **This section has provided guidelines on responses to average comments. However, some situations are difficult to deal with. The following passage gives tips to some difficult situations that researchers may encounter when submitting papers. Please read carefully and then complete the passage with words in the box.**

plain	temptation	accompanied	pushed	off
hobbyhorse	sarcastic	excisions	humble	option
hostile	addressed	scenario	skimp	adjudicate

The above are guidelines on responses to average comments. However, some situations are different and difficult to deal with. The following tips may be used.

(1) Referees with Conflicting Viewpoints

At first, this __(1)__ might appear very difficult to the novice, yet it should be viewed as a gift. You, the author, have the choice of which viewpoint you agree with the most. Then it is simply a question of playing one referee __(2)__ against the other in your reply. You can always appeal to the editor by asking him/her to make the final decision, but give them your preferred __(3)__ with reasons.

(2) The Referee Is Wrong

Referees are not Gods, but human beings who make mistakes. Sometimes they do not read your paper properly, and instead go on at length about their __(4)__ whereas in fact you have dealt with their concerns elsewhere in the paper. Try to resist the __(5)__ of rubbing their nose in it with lofty sarcastic phrases such as "If the referee had bothered to read our paper ...", but instead say something like "We agree that this is an important point and we have already __(6)__ it on Page A, Paragraph B, Line C". Sometimes the referee is just __(7)__ wrong about something. If so, it is silly to agree with the referee, and you are entitled to a good argument. If you are confident that you are right, then simply argue back with facts that can be referenced—the editor can then __(8)__ who has the best evidence on their side.

(3) The Referee Is Just Plain Rude

Anyone who has done clinical research will realize just how difficult it can be, and there is no place for rudeness from referees. It is sad that senior academics can sometimes forget their __(9)__ beginnings when they referee other's work. Nearly all journals provide clear guidance for their referees to avoid remarks which they would find hurtful if applied to their own work, yet some ignore such advice and delight in rude or __(10)__ comments, possibly as a result of envy or insecurity. In such circumstances, all you need to do is to complain to the editor and ask for another non-__(11)__ review.

(4) The Dreaded "Reduce the Paper by 30%" Request

Such a request typically comes from the editor who is __(12)__ for space in his/her journal. It is confessed that this comment is dreaded most of all because it is often __(13)__ by 3 referees' comments, the response to which usually involves making the article longer than the original submission. A general reduction in text by 30% basically requires a total rewriting (which is slow and painful). It is usually easier to make a brave decision to drop an entire section that adds little to the paper. Ask a colleague who is not involved in the paper to take out their editing knife and suggest non-essential areas that can go—even though the process of losing your precious words may seem very painful to you. Discussion sections are usually the best place to look for radical __(14)__ of entire paragraphs. Background sections should be just one or two paragraphs long—just long enough to say why the study was done, rather than an exhaustive review of all previous literature. Please do not __(15)__ on the methods section unless you are referring to a technique which can be put on a website or referenced.

Useful expressions and sentence patterns

- Thank you for your review.
- I really appreciate you bringing this issue to my attention.
- Thank you for bringing this to our attention.
- Thank you for letting us know about this. Your feedback helps us get better. We are looking into this issue and hope to resolve it promptly and accurately.
- Thank you for this important comment. To address the …, we have …
- Thank you for this suggestion. We agree on the … We have now performed … analyses to …
- This is a great comment: … We can speculate that …
- We thank for this opportunity to clarify this point. We would like to note that …

- We thank the reviewer for the query that we should also discuss trials to implement. We have now made the following revisions: ...
- We agree that ... is indeed counteracting ... However, ... The observations suggest that ... and hence ...

Delivering Opening and Closing Speeches

This chapter will provide necessary information on and practical skills in:
- Delivering opening speeches
- Delivering closing speeches
- Chairing a session

Section 1
Delivering Opening Speeches

Warm-up

The following are parts of an opening speech. Please put them in order.

(1) Nanjing University pays great attention to the international academic exchanges and cooperation, especially the exchanges and cooperation with the first-class universities in the world. We have already set up many such relationships. Today, I have had the honor of talking with the delegation from ×××University headed by Professor Smith. I hope this International Conference will pave the way for the further exchanges and cooperation between our two universities.

(2) May everyone have a pleasant stay in Nanjing!

(3) Nanjing University is one of the key universities in China, which is co-supported by the Education Ministry and the Jiangsu Provincial Government. Our university attaches great importance to researches in humanities and social sciences as well as natural sciences. The Center for XYZ Studies of our university has been actively involved in this field and has made remarkable achievements. The holding of this International Conference on XYZ studies in our university will no doubt be a new impetus to the development of our research in this area.

(4) At this opening ceremony of the XYZ Conference, please allow me to extend our warmest congratulations to the conference and our most cordial welcome to all the scholars and guests from home and abroad. It's an honor for us to have the opportunity to host this conference at Nanjing University.

(5) As is known to all, the XYZ study is …

(6) Respected Professor Smith, distinguished delegates and guests:

(7) Thank you all!

An international academic conference usually begins with the opening speech delivered by the conference secretary, the chairperson or a government official, welcoming all the conference participants and introducing the conference related activities. This section will discuss the opening speech in terms of content and style.

In terms of content, an opening speech consists of beginning, body and ending. The beginning part is usually shortened to the salutation and the greetings, and the ending part is to express thanks to the whole audience, and to announce formally the conference opening. The body part is the main part, aimed to:

(1) explain "my" (the speaker's) name, "my" role and the reason for "my" speaking here (Namely, who am "I" and why do "I" speak here?).

(2) explain the purpose, value and detailed arrangement (Specifically, why do "we" gather together for this meeting and what are the details of the meeting?).

(3) express "my" thanks to conference staff and best wishes for the conference.

Hence, the body part usually includes the following aspects:
- ✓ welcoming the participants to the conference
- ✓ showing honors and giving thanks to related parties and individuals
- ✓ introducing the history and achievements of previous conferences if any
- ✓ stating the conference purpose
- ✓ briefing the program arrangements
- ✓ expressing gratitude to conference-related parties and also best wishes for the conference

Listed below are 3 samples of opening speeches, delivered respectively by the host of the organizing committee, an official in the host city and a director of the host university. The framework of Sample 1 is displayed with annotations on the right. The rest two samples' frameworks are to be summarized by yourself.

Sample 1

Dear Colleagues:[1]	1. Salutation
On behalf of the Organizing Committee **I warmly welcome you to** the 19th International Congress of Zoology.[2] **There are** more than 50 interesting **symposia**, covering a wide range of branches of zoology such as evolution and systematics, ecology, conservation biology, reproductive biology, diseases, ethics and philosophy.[3] Some symposia will present recent advances of zoology, using modern molecular and biological techniques, some will present new discoveries and applications of traditional zoology, and others will discuss philosophy and ethics of zoology.[4] **We are honored to invite** some distinguished zoologists **to give plenary speeches.**[5] The interesting social activities and cultural tours during the conference will give you deep impression.[6]	2. Welcoming the participants 3–6. Introducing programs of the conference
In this new century, with rapid and ongoing industrialization, we face more environmental challenges than ever before: invasion of alien species, extinction of endangered species, environmental deterioration, outbreaks of diseases and pests, and so on.[7] Fortunately, we have become more capable in dealing with these challenges in the rapid development of modern zoology.[8] **I sincerely hope that participants worldwide will take this opportunity to** exchange ideas, to enhance collaboration, to establish friendships for the future of zoology, and to promote our capacity for solving the conflicts between wildlife and humans.[9]	7–8. Introducing the background of the conference 9. Introducing the conference purpose
I wish the congress will be successful and productive, **and wish you to** have a very pleasant and memorable experience in the beautiful and historical city of Beijing.[10] Thank you![11]	10. Expressing good wishes 11. Expressing thanks

Sample 2

Welcome Speech by Mr. Wang Dekun

President Davidson,[1]

Ladies and gentlemen,[1]

It is a great honor for us to have the Sixth IEEE Conference on Artificial Intelligence Applications (CAIA) held here in Nanjing, the capital of our Province.[2] **I am** Wang Dekun, mayor of Nanjing City.[3] **Please allow me on behalf of** the Jiangsu Provincial Government and myself **to extend my warmest congratulations on** the convening of this conference. **I would also like to warmly welcome you**—all the conference participants home and abroad to the conference.[4]

Jiangsu is one of the most developed provinces in China. It is known for its strength and potential for further development in industry, agriculture, science and technology, culture, education, etc. Jiangsu is such a congenial place that it attracts talented people from everywhere. Since the implementation of the policy of reform and opening, Jiangsu Province has made great and rapid advancement in various aspect of its economic and cultural life. It has also made remarkable achievements in the past few years in its exchange and cooperation with foreign countries.[5]

CAIA will no doubt be a new impetus to the development of Jiangsu, which sits in the middle between conferences that are almost purely theoretical and those that are almost purely applications oriented. The **purpose** of this conference is to educate the professional software engineer in how to apply AI techniques to real problems. **We are honored to invite** some distinguished experts **to give keynote speeches**, focusing on the boundary between theory and practice; in particular, on representations and problem-solving techniques and their demonstrated application to real problems. Consequently, there is a conjoint emphasis on "what" (the application) and "how" (the method). **Thus, CAIA will provide the opportunity** for researchers and engineers who are interested in "real world" applications to share their ideas and experiences.[6]

I sincerely applaud the opening of this conference, which is **indeed a platform of technological exchange** for guest experts and scholars home and abroad. I believe, by way of this conference, the relationship between us will be strengthened and we will innovate more beneficial solutions through the use of artificial intelligence technologies.[7]

I would like all of you to feel at home here in China and **wish the conference a great success.**[8]

Thank you.[9]

1. _____
2. _____
3. _____
4. _____
5. _____
6. _____
7. _____
8. _____
9. _____

Sample 3

Language and the Scientific Imagination: Proceedings of the 11th Conference of the International Society for the Study of European Ideas (ISSEI), 28 July – 2 August 2008 at the Language Centre, University of Helsinki, Finland.

Distinguished Conference Delegates,[1]
Ladies and gentlemen,[1]

It gives me great pleasure to welcome you all to Finland, to Helsinki and to the University of Helsinki.[2]

The University of Helsinki and its Language Centre **are proud to have been given the opportunity to** organize the eleventh international conference of the International Society for the Study of European Ideas.[3] The **topic** of the conference this year is "Language and the Scientific Imagination".[4]

A succession of conferences of any given organization has sometimes been compared to a caravan.[5] The caravan moves on, things get unpacked and then packed up again, and the camp site changes from one to the next.[6] It is always on the move, always changing, always on a quest for new approaches, new dialogue, new ground, new friends.[7]

To give you an idea about the present camp site, **let me briefly introduce** the University of Helsinki to you.[8]

The University of Helsinki is, by all accounts (and at the moment, according to those fashionable university rankings), **the top university** in Finland and one of the leading multidisciplinary research universities in Europe.[9] Not even modesty—so characteristic of the Finnish people—prevents me from stating this obvious fact. Quite uniquely, the **history** of the University of Helsinki also reflects the history of Finland as a nation, the position of Finnish and Swedish as the two national languages, and the rise of national identity in general.[10]

The University was founded in 1640 by Queen Christina of Sweden as the Royal Academy of Turku—Turku being a city some 200 kilometers from Helsinki on the southwest coast of Finland.[11] At that time, Finland was part of Sweden.[12] The Royal Academy of Turku had four faculties, a few hundred students, extensive autonomy and a right to levy taxes from farms and parishes.[13] Teaching was given in Latin, although Swedish was gaining ground in the late 18th century.[14]

From 1809, following the fall of Finland to a Russian regime, the Royal Academy was turned into the Imperial Academy of Turku, with

1. _____
2. _____
3. _____
4. _____
5 – 7. _____
8 – 36. _____

the Grand Duke of Russia as Chancellor.[15] The Academy moved from Turku to Helsinki in 1828 and became the Imperial Alexander University (after the Grand Duke Alexander).[16] Swedish replaced Latin as the language of tuition—Finnish gaining ground in the late 19th century.[17] With the newly gained independence, the Imperial Alexander University then became the University of Helsinki in 1919.[18]

We are now in **the Main Building of the University**.[19] You may have noticed the square in front of this building—an important part of the historical milieu of the city.[20] The square is surrounded by three sources of power, if you will—the spiritual represented by the church, the secular by the government building, and the arts and sciences or the academic world embodied in the University Main Building.[21] It seems to me that this setting emphasizes the autonomy of the University in a symbolic and beautiful manner.[22]

The history of the University is also reflected in this Great Hall. The lectern or teacher's desk where I am standing now dates back to Turku Academy.[23] It was made in Stockholm in 1814 and is said to be the most valuable piece of university furniture in the Nordic countries.[24] The doors of this Great Hall as well go back to the year 1814.[25]

Today, **the University** of Helsinki is **a large institution** with 11 faculties, more than 38 000 students, close to 8,000 staff members and a budget of over half a billion euros.[26] The University operates on four campuses in Helsinki and in 19 other locations in Finland.[27] Out of the 20 universities in Finland, the "market share" of the University of Helsinki in 2007 is impressive: it receives approximately one fourth of the country's budget funding for universities, it has one fourth of its professors and produces one fourth of its doctoral degrees.[28] Sixty-one percent of the national centers of excellence are situated here.[29]

A member of the League of European Research Universities, LERU, the University of Helsinki has **wide scientific contacts** all around the world and a vision to enlarge the number of its international students and staff rapidly.[30] The university is bilingual, with teaching in both national languages, Finnish and Swedish. To a growing extent, tuition is also given in English.[31]

The Language Centre of the University, **your conference host**, is an institute of 250 language professionals, giving language tuition to all university students in the two national languages and foreign languages, 16 languages in all, and providing high quality language services for both university and outside customers.[32]

But enough of facts and figures. I am sure you are suitably impressed already (and have forgiven me for being so wordy about it

all). [33] What we would like you to remember this camp site, the University of Helsinki, not by figures and statistics, but by the hospitable and friendly atmosphere of the University and its staff, the lively discussions at the workshops and panel discussions, the beautiful surroundings and the good organisation of the conference. [34] A successful conference is not only about intellectual stimulation and the meeting of minds. [35] It is also—and maybe more importantly—about meeting old friends and gaining new ones. [36]	
Organising a large conference is a joint effort. **I would like to take this opportunity to thank all our partners in this undertaking, in particular** the co-chairs of the conference, Dr Ezra Talmor and Dr Marja Härmänmaa with her crew. [37] Without your dedication and excellent cooperation, we would not be here today. [38]	37 – 38. _____
Ladies and Gentlemen: the patron of this conference is the President of the Republic of Finland, Ms Tarja Halonen. [39] She has sent the following message to the conference and its participants, and I will take this opportunity to read her message to you. [40] MESSAGE FROM THE PRESIDENT OF THE REPUBLIC OF FINLAND [41] *The 11th ISSEI Conference is a remarkable example of the possibilities for global research collaboration.* [42] *The examination of and support for cooperation between humanities and sciences form an important element in understanding and developing European societies.* [43] *I wish all the participants a successful week and fruitful discussions.* [44] *I hope that the sharing of ideas will lead to new knowledge and vision.* [45]	39 – 45. _____
On behalf of the University of Helsinki and the Language Centre: **welcome to** Helsinki, **and enjoy the conference!** [46]	46. _____

In accord with the conference purpose and the theme, the opening speech of an international academic conference tends to be formal, which is embodied in the usage of technical terms, noun compounds, nominalization, long, compound and complex sentences, etc.

However, opening speeches at academic conferences also have some colloquial features, e. g., the use of the 1st and 2nd persons, colloquial expressions, body language, etc., which aim to close the distance between the speaker and the audience, and to create a friendly and harmonious atmosphere.

Though the conference opening speeches are similar in content, they are slightly different when given by speakers with different titles and standing points, which is well illustrated by the above 3 samples.

Exercises

❶ Read the above three samples, and discuss with your partner about the structure of each one. Then identify the sentences or expressions with stylistic features.

		Sample 1	Sample 2	Sample 3
Structure	Beginning	Sentences __ to __	Sentences __ to __	Sentences __ to __
	Body	Sentences __ to __	Sentences __ to __	Sentences __ to __
	Ending	Sentences __ to __	Sentences __ to __	Sentences __ to __
Stylistic features	technical terms: _____ noun compounds: _____ nominalization: _____ long, compound and complex sentences: _____ 1st person: _____ 2nd person: _____ colloquial expressions: _____			

The following are references of sentence patterns and phrases for opening speeches:

(1) **Salutation**

➤ Honorable Chairman, President *** and distinguished guests

➤ Dr/Professor ***, Dr./Professor ***, ladies and gentlemen

➤ Mr. Chairman, fellow delegates, ladies and gentlemen

➤ Distinguished conference delegates

➤ Ladies and gentlemen

(2) **Announcing the Opening of the Conference**

➤ I'd like to call the conference to order. / May I have your attention, please? / Please be seated. / Shall we get down to business?

➤ It's time to begin our session. / I am very pleased/honored/delighted to declare the Conference open.

(3) **Making a Self-Introduction**

➤ My name is *** from New York University. I am going to chair / I will be responsible for this morning's conference / panel session / parallel session. I declare now the opening of the conference on …

(4) **Welcoming the Participants**

➤ As the chairperson of the conference, I am honored to have this opportunity to welcome you to the conference.

➢ With a profound feeling of pleasure and privilege, I will speak on behalf of the Organizing Committee of this conference to extend the heartiest welcome to all of you here.

➢ You have come all the way for this conference. Thank you very much for your participation!

➢ On behalf of the (*WCC 2000 Organizing Committee*) and (*the Ministry of Information Industry*), I am very pleased to warmly welcome (*experts, professionals and entrepreneurs of the IT Industry from various countries around the word*) to attend this great trans-century gathering.

➢ It is my pleasure to welcome (*the global community of researchers, policy makers and health industry representatives*) to the Annual Meeting of (*Health Technology Assessment International 2022*).

➢ On behalf of the Organizing Committee, I would like to welcome all members, guests and spouses to this special event for what will certainly be an exciting, enjoyable and educational experience.

(5) **Introducing Conference Topics and Programs**

➢ There are more than 50 interesting symposia, covering a wide range of branches of (*zoology such as evolution and systematics, ecology, conservation biology, reproductive biology, diseases, ethics and philosophy*).

➢ A wide range of exciting and cutting-edge topics, including (*classical protein chemistry, novel proteomic technologies, information gained on functional subproteomes and applications in human disease, and investigations utilizing animal and plant models*) will be covered in various formats including workshops, speaker sessions and poster sessions.

➢ The meeting will tackle the key questions of (*assessing quality, effectiveness, and appropriateness of not only medical devices, equipment, and pharmaceuticals, but all procedures and processes for prevention, treatment and rehabilitation*), as well as (*assessments in the public health context and in regard to systems and organizational issues*).

➢ Topics to be presented will include: (*Biomechanics, Biomaterials & Nanotechnology, Artificial Organs, and Neuromuscular Control, etc.*)

➢ The scientific program includes the traditional plenary session symposia and poster sessions.

➢ Besides the scientific program, a social program for the participants will give you an opportunity to discover Lisbon with the abundance of its historical sites and beautiful scenery ...

(6) Introducing Conference Purposes/Aims

➤ This conference is to share our experience and knowledge in regard to the theory, new developments, and possible applications of these two promising techniques.

➤ To this end it is very gratifying to me that we are assembled here today for an informative exchange of ideas.

➤ The aim/goal of this conference is threefold / has three objectives / is to secure three objectives. Firstly, it should provide a forum for the exchange of information between participants in this interdisciplinary meeting. Secondly, it should provide an opportunity to establish and renew personal relationships between participants. And finally, it should stimulate the interest and ambition of participants.

➤ It is the aim of this conference to bring together mainly those who have contributed over a period of years to this subject. Our purpose here is to define the present status of knowledge concerning ### in five different fields. Firstly ... Secondly ... Thirdly ... Fourthly ... Finally ...

➤ I hope that this 6th International Conference of ### will improve our understanding of ###. I also hope that the conference will provide the opportunity for personal exchange of scientific results, facilitate the making of new acquaintances, and promote personal friendship among participants.

➤ We hope you will be enriched, stimulated, and greatly enjoy this excellent program (*that highlights scientific psychology and its applications in all areas of the discipline*).

➤ The congress aims to showcase the progress of (*proteomic sciences and related disciplines*), to promote global collaboration, and to cultivate a new generation of scientists.

➤ This congress offers a great opportunity for international scientists to share their accomplishments and knowledge with their Chinese colleagues, and to take a look at the stunning changes in science and other aspects of life in China.

➤ (*The World Congress for Chinese Biochemical Engineers 2022*) will be a memorable event for our Chinese colleagues and friends from all over the world to establish friendship, to promote academic exchanges at an international level, and to promote the interests of (*Chinese biomedical engineers*).

(7) **Introducing Conference History**

➢ (*The International Association for Cross-Cultural Psychology*) was founded in Hong Kong in 1972. It has undertaken 16 congresses in many countries of the world in over 30 years.

➢ Fourteen months ago, the International Conference on Information Technology and Application was successfully held in Australia and this paved the way for this year's meeting.

➢ (*Dentist Tech China*) has experienced its eight years in China and achieved a great success in 2003. It has become one of the most important (*dental events*) in China.

➢ Started in 1994, this event is the first of its kind and has been wholly supported by (*the local government, public health organizations, and associations*).

➢ (*The Human Proteome Organization*) has had two previous annual international congresses, the first in France and the second in Canada. These congresses brought together scientists from both academia and industry for networking and establishing collaboration.

(8) **Expressing Good Wishes**

➢ Now I wish the conference a great success. May everyone a pleasure stay in Shanghai. Thank you all!

➢ I would like all of you to feel at home here in Beijing. Now I would like to conclude my speech by wishing the conference a complete success. Thank you!

➢ I am sure that this conference will offer you an opportunity for forging personal ties with one another, and above all, to exchange results, ideas and projects from which future progress will develop.

➢ I wish the congress will be successful and productive, and wish you have a very pleasant and memorable experience in the beautiful and historical city of Beijing.

➢ I hope that you will have a scientifically and socially productive experience in Beijing.

➢ I wish that (*Dentist Tech China 2022*) will be another successful and fruitful event.

➢ I wish every success for this conference. I wish all the participants enjoy their visit to our university, and enjoy their life in Shanghai.

➢ Please accept my best wishes for a successful and rewarding conference.

➢ We are confident that you will enjoy the science, the warm friendship and the rich cultural activities in Beijing.

➤ Hope this event will be your firm step to (*penetrate the huge Chinese dental market*).

❷ **The paragraphs are adapted from an opening speech addressed by Anne Husebekk, rector of UiT, the Arctic University of Norway. Read the paragraphs carefully and put them in the right order.**

(1) Digitalization is an aspect of research (and education) that will be increasingly important, and I am proud to say that even though Norway is a bit of a "slow starter" in this field, UiT is at the national forefront, and an active partner in international collaboration.

(2) Digital Tools in Music Technology Education and the Wittgenstein Archives are two of the other initiatives that will be presented—as will be the CLARIN and DARIAH research infrastructures, both of which UiT participate in.

(3) The Norwegian Historical Data Centre, a national institution hosted by the Faculty of Humanities, Social Science and Education working to computerize Norwegian censuses from 1865 onwards, as well as parish registers and other sources from the 18th and 19th centuries. In effect this will build a national population registry from 1800 to the present day—a unique tool for further research.

(4) With this, I hope you will all have productive discussions, and I wish you a productive day of the conference!

(5) Welcoming guests to a conference hosted by UiT is one of my favorite things to do as rector! It is a clear and concrete manifestation of one of the most important things that we as academics do; presenting the most recent knowledge in a field of research, and discussing these findings with colleagues from around the world.

(6) I am particularly happy (and proud!) that you've had the opportunity to learn more about some of the projects in this field here at UiT.

(7) Giellatekno, Centre for Saami language technology at the University of Tromso, where cutting-edge linguistic and computational research on the analysis of Saami and other morphologically-rich languages is combined with the development of practical applications, such as dictionaries or translation software.

(8) Dear participants at the UiT Digital Humanities Conference!

❸ **Prepare a welcome speech with reference to the information given in the table below, and deliver it to the whole class.**

Conference	the 28th International Congress of Psychology
Uniqueness	• the first International Congress of Psychology to be held in a developing Asian county • providing a special opportunity for exchanges in all areas of psychology, and among different cultures of the world
Host city	• Beijing • a thriving center for contemporary scientific, technological and business advances; an example of global confluence and exchanges
Contributions	bringing together distinguished psychologists at a large international congress; providing an opportunity to discuss how psychology can contribute to mankind and a safer world
Supporter	the Chinese Academy of Sciences
Purpose	be enriched, stimulated by, and greatly enjoy an excellent program that highlights scientific psychology and its applications in all areas of the discipline

❹ **Translate the following welcome speech into English.**

上海,东方的璀璨之都,有着与当今世界相交融的现代文明,有着蓬勃生机和无限活力。在这个充满希望的城市里,我们上海隧道工程股份有限公司(Shanghai Tunnel Engineering Construction Co. Ltd)很荣幸地与上海土木工程协会(Shanghai Society of Civil Engineering)、上海城市建设研究院(Shanghai Urban Construction Design & Research Institute)、同济大学(Tongji University)等联合举办2003上海国际隧道工程研讨会(Shanghai International Symposium on Tunnel Engineering)。我谨代表组委会向与会的国内外专家学者致以热情的欢迎。

近十年来,随着中国经济的迅猛发展,中国的交通隧道建设取得了举世瞩目的成就。作为中国最有活力的城市之一,上海一直把改善交通基础设施建设作为发展经济的重点,在交通基础设施建设上投以巨资。城市交通隧道作为城市基础设施建设的重要组成部分,其影响和作用将会越来越大。根据上海远景规划,城市交通隧道的建设还将大规模增加,这对上海城市交通隧道的建设与管理提出了更高的要求,也为我们之间的交流与合作提供了更广阔的前景。

本次研讨会为国内外专家学者提供了技术交流的舞台。我相信通过本次研讨会,我们之间的联系将进一步加强,彼此间的合作和友谊将得到进一步发展。

最后,祝各位代表在上海生活工作愉快,祝大会圆满成功!

❺ Online academic conferences are increasingly popular since the outbreak of COVID-19. Scan the QR code and watch the opening speech given by Professor Rong Zeng in Tsinghua University. Discuss with your partners whether the procedure or schedule of the online opening speech is similar to or different from the offline ones.

Section 2
Delivering Closing Speeches

Warm-up

1. What is the function of a conference closing speech?
2. Who is likely to be designated to deliver a conference closing speech?
3. What are the components of a conference closing speech?

An international academic conference concludes with a closing speech, which is normally given by the conference chairperson, a prestigious scholar or a government official. The style of the closing speech is similar to that of the opening speech.

In terms of content, a closing speech also consists of the beginning, the body and the ending. The beginning part is shortened to the salutation and greetings, and the ending part is to give thanks and to formally announce the conference closure and the date of the next congress if any. The body part is the main part, aimed to:

- Explain "my" (the speaker's) name, "my" role and the reason for "my" speaking here. Namely, who am "I" and why do "I" speak here?
- Explain the outcome and the achievements of the conference. Specifically, how many attendees have come to the conference, how many presentations have been given, what are the rewarding viewpoints created?
- Express "my" thanks to conference staff and all the participants for their devotion to the conference success.

Hence, the body part usually includes the following aspects:
✓ Showing honors to be designated to speak
✓ Making a general introduction to conference activities and achievements
✓ Looking to the future development and application prospects
✓ Expressing sincere thanks to the efforts of conference staff and participants, and sending wishes of a pleasant return trip
✓ Announcing the date of the next congress if any

The following are 3 samples of closing speeches. The framework of Sample 1 is displayed with annotations on the right. The rest two samples' frameworks are to be summarized by yourself.

Sample 1 　　Your Royal Highness, 　　Mr. President of New York University, 　　Dear friends and colleagues, 　　Ladies and gentlemen,[1] 　　**First of all, I would like to thank** President William Brown and the Organizing Committee for having appointed me to serve as the General Chair of this Conference.[2] 　　We are now very close to the end of the 7th International Conference of Thermodynamics which has achieved tremendous successes. More than 200 participants have come to Manhattan to discuss not only general questions about thermodynamics but more concrete questions and problems and their possible solutions.[3] 　　230 participants is **a strong signal of** belonging, support and involvement on which future activities can be built. Local and regional authorities are backbones of society and this has been very clear also during this conference.[4] 　　We **have worked actively in** the workshops these days and our work has provided value not only to the resolution but also to the work of the Association of Thermodynamics in general. **Therefore**, I can thoroughly say that **the resolution and contributions** from the workshops presented these days reflect the position of Association of Thermodynamics based on the opinions of its member regions and will form the basis for the future work of our Association.[5] 　　I shall end here by **thanking** you **for** coming to the 7th International Conference of Thermodynamics. I hope that you have benefited much from the conference and from discussions with colleagues.[6]	1. **Salutation** 2. **Extending thanks to the organizers** 3. **Congratulating on the success of the conference** 4-5. **Summarizing the achievements** 6-11. **Extending thanks to participants, organizers, etc.**

Once again **I thank my** friend Bill **for** inviting us to this beautiful city.[7] **Thank you to** New York University for hosting the conference.[8] **Thank you to** everybody who has contributed to the conference with reports and introductions.[9] **Thank you for** the financial contributions to this conference from the city and all other organizations and a number of private sponsors.[10] And last but not least, **thank you to Mr.** James Raven and Mrs. Michiko Ayukawa for the overall organizing of the conference.[11] And lastly, my friends, **see you next year** in Beijing, China **for** our **next conference**.[12] **I wish** everybody a pleasant and safe journey home.[13] **Thank you all!**[14]	12. **Inviting people to the next conference** 13. **Good wishes** 14. **Expressing thanks**

Sample 2

Madam Chairperson, Your Excellencies, Honorable Ministers, Distinguished delegates, Colleagues, Ladies and gentlemen,[1] **On behalf of** the Office of the Special Advisor to the Secretary General on Gender Issues and the Advancement of Women, **I wish to express my thanks for** the opportunity to make a statement at the closing session of the very successful 7th African Regional Conference for Women. **I wish to thank** the Government and the people of Ethiopia, **for** looking after us so well and making us feel welcomed in every way. **Our sincere gratitude goes to Mr.** Amoako, Executive Secretary of ECA, **for** facilitating this conference and for enabling joint sessions with the Fourth Africa Development Forum as well as the Commission on HIV/AIDS and Governance in Africa.[2]	1. _____ 2. _____

We are all indebted to Ms. Josephine Ouedraogo, the Director of the African Center for Gender and Development at the ECA, **and** her **team, for** their tireless efforts in catering to so many of our needs so that we can accomplish what we came to do here. The preparation, organization, management and coordination of all the various processes of a conference of this magnitude is no easy task. We commend your leadership and the commitment of your entire staff.³

Madam Chairperson,

I do not wish to repeat what so many have said so eloquently at this conference in setting the agenda to promote the **achievement** of gender equality and the empowerment of women in Africa. Achievements over the ten years since the Dakar and the Beijing Platforms for Action were adopted **have been lauded, gaps have been identified and the lessons** we have learned **have been shared and discussed.**⁴

But there are new aspects of this conference which seem to signal that in order to achieve gender equality in Africa, all of us—that is governments, the civil society and the development partners—recognize that we must cease doing things in the usual manner.⁵

Madame Chairperson,

In conclusion, let me congratulate you and the members of your Bureau for taking on the leadership for the Africa regional women's agenda emanating from this conference. Your election and that of your team is richly deserved.⁶

I look forward to seeing many of you in New York in March 2025. At that time, you will meet with yet another African woman leader. Ms. Rachel Manyanja from Uganda who has been appointed by the UN Secretary General as the new Assistant Secretary General for Gender Issues and the Advancement of Women.⁷

For now, **I wish you all a safe journey back home.**⁸

Thank you for your attention.⁹

3. _____

4-5. _____

6. _____

7. _____

8. _____
9. _____

Sample 3

Your Royal Highness, Mr. President of the Chulalongkorn University, Dear colleagues, Ladies and gentlemen,[1]	1. Salutation
Dear Mercedes, I shall be very short. **I only want to say three things**.[2]	2. _____
Firstly, I am very happy with the success of this Conference. Not only were we delighted and honored to have such a nice first morning so kindly presided over by Her Royal Highness, Princess Maha Chakri Sirindhorn, **but also two plenary debates** that were quite attractive and lively, and very interesting regular sessions. **The high quality of the scientific contents of these sessions demonstrates that** Asian population studies are going well, and that international exchanges on these topics can be fruitful in this part of the world. I can tell you that at least the sessions I have been able to attend consisted of high quality paper presentations, serious discussions of the papers, and lively and active participation from the floor. And I was told that it was the same in most other sessions. **I would like to congratulate all of you, and also to thank you**, because this success is even more of a success if we take into account the difficulties encountered because of a tight conference budget, **I would especially thank all who** worked so much and so well in spite of lack of support, including those participants who accepted reduced travel allowances or did their best to find their own travel support.[3]	3. _____
Secondly, I would like to thank again everybody who contributed to the organization of this first South-East Asian Conference. Indeed, I would like to thank again those institutions which made the conference possible by providing financial support.[4]	4. _____
But **I would particularly like to thank everybody who gave so much of their time and their energy to organize the conference**. On the Thai side, so many people acted so efficiently that you will forgive me for not acknowledging each of them. But I do want to express my gratitude to scholars, students and staff of the Chulalongkorn University, the College for Population Studies and the Thai Population Association. I want to express my personal thanks to Vipan Prachuabmoh and Nappapor Chayovan who mobilized so efficiently all the forces of these institutions. I can tell them that IUSSP is deeply grateful to them and through them to so many people who participated in the National Organizing Committee and contributed to the impressive organization of this successful conference.[5]	5. _____

Finally, I would like to express to you, dear Mercedes, **my very sincere congratulations and warm thanks for** having chaired so kindly and so successfully the International Organizing Committee.⁶	6. _____
My third point will be very brief. **I am simply delighted to invite** all of you and all of your Asian colleagues interested in population studies to prepare **to come to** France in a couple of years **to participate** in the 2025 IUSSP General Conference. I still cannot tell you exactly where that conference will take place. It may be Montpelier, Tours, Nantes or elsewhere. Whatever the place, I hope very much that France 2025 will be as successful as Bangkok 2020!⁷	7. _____
I cannot close without thanking all of you again who have participated in this conference. So, thanks to everybody, and please come to France in 2025. You will be warmly received there!⁸	8. _____

Exercises

❶ Read the above three samples, and discuss with your partner about the structure of each one. Then identify the sentences or expressions with stylistic features of academic conference closing speeches.

		Sample 1	Sample 2	Sample 3
Structure	Beginning	Sentences __ to __	Sentences __ to __	Sentences __ to __
	Body	Sentences __ to __	Sentences __ to __	Sentences __ to __
	Ending	Sentences __ to __	Sentences __ to __	Sentences __ to __
Stylistic features	technical terms: _____ noun compounds: _____ nominalization: _____ long, compound and complex sentences: _____ 1st person: _____ 2nd person: _____ colloquial expressions: _____			

The following are examples of sentence patterns and phrases used in closing speeches:

(1) **Declaring the End of the Conference**

➢ We are soon closing this seminar which has been a great success.

➢ We have come to the end of this interesting and productive conference.

➢ Our historic conference, the First Conference of (*Legal Chancellors and*

> *Ombudsmen of the Nordic and Baltic Countries*) is coming to an end.
> We are now very close to the end of the (*3rd Conference of the International Carnivorous Plant Society*).
> Now with great joy and a mind reluctant to part, we get together again to declare that the Conference has drawn to a successful close.
> Now the conference is closed. Let's meet again in London in 2026.
> Mr. Chairman, Governors, honored guests, we come to the end of a very fruitful set of meetings.

(2) **Commenting on the Conference**
> Firstly, I am very happy with the success of this conference.
> Let me congratulate you on the achievements of this conference.
> Please accept my congratulations on a successful conference.
> This conference was a success because the proceedings were conducted in a respectful and dignified manner, the two fundamental conditions for the establishment of a dialogue.
> The conference was a success as a direct result of the great support it received from a great number of people.
> I am very encouraged by the success of this conference. This event has demonstrated that as a state we can all come together to share our resources, ideas, and thoughts as we continue to make a collective effort to guarantee that each student has a chance to succeed.
> Let me begin by thanking you for a wonderfully informative and efficient Oxford conference. I really enjoyed it!
> Certainly, the conference has been very successful in (*bringing out issues and in highlighting some of the pertinent aspects of plantation development*).
> In light of the specific objectives of this three-day Conference, I should confess that this is a successful one as far as the lessons learned and sharing of information are concerned.
> From our side we can only say that everything was successful, professional and especially we foreigners have been receiving the most wonderful Chinese hospitality.

(3) **Summarizing Conference Achievements**
> We have been listening to 11 presentations selected out of 38 which were printed in the Proceedings. To have such a program all in one day is a heavy task but in this case it has been really worth the effort.

> Despite all of the inevitable small difficulties, there have been, you will agree, a number of thoughtful and probing contributions in plenary sessions, and many first-rate seminars and roundtables on an infinite number of subjects.

> It is heartwarming that the presentations and discussions during the past three days showed that (*there are indeed enough mechanisms, enough approaches to make management of forestry sustainable*).

> We talked a lot, we discussed a lot and we also recommended a lot of things numbering at least fourteen concrete suggestions.

> In the past few days you have been addressing themes of paramount importance, and please allow me to express my admiration and appreciation of your wisdom in these fields, since such wisdom is the basis for action.

> I believe that our conference has been a great success. It went smoothly as scheduled. In these five days the conference has covered so many important and complex problems in the field of (*applied linguistics*), both theoretical and practical.

> Several interesting aspects of (*logistics practices*) were presented by keynote speakers at the plenary sessions.

> The presentation of paper took place in three parallel sessions covering eight different topics in (*logistics*), (*although there were a large number of papers and time pressure*).

> The audience attended and participated with great interest in learning the results of research by scientists and business experts.

> Questions and discussions flowed and triggered ideas for future research and applications, whereas the exchange of opinions and the acquaintances made among participants have formed the basis for future cooperation between them.

> There were nearly 350 attendees to the conference. The large number helped provide a nice audience for each of the technical sessions.

> We originally hoped to draw about 150 people to the event, I am happy to report that we exceeded our original goal.

(4) **Expressing Feelings**

> Let me give you a brief summary of the feelings which I have now about this seminar: …

> It has truly been inspiring to be here and listen to all the experiences and viewpoints that have been raised from so many different parts of the world.

➢ All the presentations were very illuminating and informative. And the heated panel discussions were very stimulating and fruitful.

➢ I felt a very good working spirit among all the delegates with a view to (*converging towards the solution of urgent telecommunication development problems and in particular to reducing the infrastructure gaps*).

➢ Although we have been here just for three days, I'm sure all of us will be carrying very happy memories of this visit to the Philippines. Many of us might not have the opportunity to really see the country but this workshop alone will make this visit always memorable.

➢ We were able to focus our thinking and interact at many different levels with other groups.

➢ We all hope to maintain close contact and cooperation with each other in future research work.

(5) Expressing Thanks to Organizers

➢ I want to thank everybody who took part in the organization of this event.

➢ Again, let me thank you very much for the great conference that you organized. I have learned a lot and was particularly pleased to meet so many interesting friends I could talk to.

➢ I want to thank you both for organizing such a successful meeting, not only for me but also for the other members of my laboratory. Of course, I would like to express my appreciation to (*DEMR*) for the fabulous job of organizing and supporting this conference.

➢ Thanks again for putting on such a super meeting. I learned a lot and had a great time.

➢ I am grateful to our hosts, (*the Government of the United Arab Emirates and the authorities of Dubai*), for their superb organizing and for providing these magnificent facilities.

(6) Expressing Thanks to Other Supporters

➢ I would also like to thank the associated institutions and organizational partners of this conference who helped us to make known and to implement the project.

➢ With regard to our collaboration with other partners in organizing this conference, I appreciate very much the efforts of my colleague at ITTO Dr. ***.

➢ As the organizers of the conference, I would like to express our sincere

thanks to the members of the international committee and the authorities of the University for all their support and contributions to this successful conference.
- But of course, as Professor *** mentioned, there has behind the scene been a nice organizing team of support staff. (*These folks worked tirelessly and many still have smiles on their faces*). They deserve another round of applause and appreciation.

(7) Expressing Thanks to Participants
- And finally, I would like to thank all presenters and participants.
- Firstly, many thanks to everyone that attended the seminar. You made our first seminar a great success.
- This conference is a success because of your efforts and participation. Thank you very much!
- On behalf of (*Secretary ****), I would like to thank all the participants for their successful contributions to this historic conference.
- Thank you for having traveled such a long distance and for having made this conference a success.
- Again, I want to thank everyone for making the (23rd DASC) an outstanding success!
- Thanks are also due to all the participants who came from over 30 countries and regions.

(8) Expressing Thanks to Presenters
- I would like to thank all of the presenters and participants who shared their expertise to make this conference a success.
- The greatest thanks go to the speakers, without whom there would have been no such conference; you were amazingly great. Many of you came over great distances at your own expense to participate, and many contributed their fees back to the conference. Everyone learned and gained from your presentations.
- Furthermore, my thanks and acknowledgments are due to all our guest speakers and reporters who through their knowledge and experience have contributed to our reflections and have generated rich debates in our work sessions.

(9) Expressing Thanks to Chairpersons
- Finally, I would like to express to you, (*Dear ****), my very sincere congratulations and warm thanks for having chaired so kindly and so

successfully the International Organizing Committee.
- ➢ I would again express my appreciation for the session chairmen. Thank you, you did an excellent job even if everybody did not have the opportunity to speak.
- ➢ And I would also like to thank Chairman *** for his able chairmanship.
- ➢ Let me congratulate you on the achievements of this conference. This was the result of very hard work by delegates under the very competent leadership of the Chairman (*Mr.* ***). I attribute this success to all the other members of the Steering Committee as well as Chairmen and Vice-Chairmen of Committees and Working Groups and thank them for their efficient work.

(10) **Inviting for the Next Conference**
- ➢ I am simply delighted to invite all of you and all of your Asian colleagues interested in population studies to prepare to come to France in a couple of years to participate in the 2025 IUSSP General Conference.
- ➢ I look forward to seeing many of you in New York in March 2025.
- ➢ Our next conference will be held in Dalian. We will try our best to make the forthcoming gathering another fruitful and pleasant one. I'm looking forward to meeting you then.
- ➢ So, thanks to everybody and, please come to China in 2025. You will be warmly received!
- ➢ The next conference will be held in Beijing in June, 2025. I hope we can meet again then and share our experience in (*Artificial Intelligence*).

(11) **Expressing Good Wishes**
- ➢ Thank you. I wish you a pleasant trip home, and I will see you again.
- ➢ I wish you a safe journey home and our thanks to the Turkish staff who have cooperated so efficiently throughout this conference.
- ➢ I wish everybody a good journey home.
- ➢ For now, I wish you all a safe journey back home.
- ➢ And lastly, my friends, see you next year in Shanghai and have a safe trip home.

❷ **The following are different parts of a closing speech. Read carefully and put them in the right order.**

(1) We all have enjoyed the advanced professional program, since we have listened to 25 presentations selected of 40 in the Proceedings in two days. They not only describe problems, but also offer solutions; they shine a light

along a dark path and offer hope that we can solve those problems. More than that, they renew our zeal and refresh our commitment. I am happy to say that this conference has been of the best type. Moreover, I, as well as all the others, enjoyed greatly the chance to visit PLA University of Science and Technology. We have talked and exchanged ideas with each other in the field of Computer Science. I have made friends with these prominent scientists and experts from different countries. And we are also deeply impressed by visiting your laboratories and research centers.

(2) The next conference will be held in our university—the University of Iowa, USA. We will try our best to make the forthcoming gathering another fruitful and pleasant one. I am looking forward to meeting you then. Thank you!

(3) Mr. Chairman, your excellencies, ladies and gentlemen,

(4) Please allow me to avail myself of this opportunity to express our heartfelt gratitude to you again.

(5) It gives me great pleasure to speak on behalf of all the participants in this closing session of the conference. We would like to first of all thank the Computer Science Society of China and the Computer Science School of PLA University of Science and Technology for your kind invitation to attend the conference which has been a great success.

❸ **Translate the following sentences into English.**

(1) 我代表组委会向各位代表为研讨会的成功举办所做的努力和贡献表示衷心的感谢。

(2) 我宣布第三届世界珠算心算联合会(Conference of the World Association of Abacus and Mental Arithmetic)大会胜利闭幕。

(3) 这次大会取得圆满成功,要归功于来自世界各地的专家学者的参与,很多人不远万里自费来参会。你们的发言令所有出席者受益匪浅。

(4) 女士们、先生们！我们成果丰硕的大会就要结束了。

(5) 下一届国际生物物理大会(International Biophysics Congress)将于2024年10月在北京召开，我期待着与大家再次相聚！

(6) 我谨代表中国中华临床医药学会(Chinese Clinical Medical & Pharmaceutical Association)，衷心感谢各位专家和研究生同学对会议的参与！

(7) 此次会议的成功举办还得到了学校人文学院(the School of Humanities)的大力支持。我代表社会心理学会(the Social Psychology Association)就你们对大会的支持和贡献表示诚挚的谢意。

(8) 本次会议到会代表125人，有13人次做了大会(plenary)报告、18个专题研讨会(symposia)、16个学术讨论会(workshop)，33人做口头发言(oral presentation)，会议讨论了生物物理学领域内许多重要的理论与实践问题。

❹ **Refer to the hints given in the blanks and complete the following closing speech.**

> Mr. Chairman, honored guests,
>
> We (1)（表示会议即将结束）_____ a very fruitful Congress. I (2)（表示谢意）_____ our hosts and the authorities of the University, for their superb organization and for providing these magnificent facilities. (3)（还要表示感谢）_____ hard-working and dedicated staff, for making these meetings possible. And I (4)（也要表示感谢）_____ Professor John Smith for his able chairmanship.
>
> The Congress started officially yesterday and was supported by the presence of political, governmental, and academic members who stressed the importance of logistics and their implementation challenges in a global environment.
>
> Several interesting aspects of logistics practices were (5)_____ （做讲演）keynote speakers at the plenary sessions. The presentation of papers took place in three parallel sessions (6)_____（涉及范围为）eight different topics in logistics. Although there were a large number of papers and time pressure, the audience (7)_____（出席参与）with great interest in learning the results of research of the scientists and business experts. Questions and discussions followed and triggered ideas for future research and applications, whereas the (8)_____（交流）of opinions and the (9)_____（结识）of the participants formed the basis for future cooperation between them.
>
> In closing, Mr. Chairman, allow me to thank all the participants for enriching these meetings with their presence and their views. I (10)_____（盼望）making progress on all of the issues we discussed at our meetings next year in Wuhan City under the chairmanship of Allen Smith.

Section 3
Chairing a Session

Warm-up

1. Is the conference chairperson the same person as the session chairperson?
2. What is the routine job of a session chairperson?

After the conference opening ceremony, various sessions of presentations and exchanges will be held, in which the session chairpersons play a big role. The session chairpersons' tasks are diverse and complex, including calling the meeting to order, introducing himself/herself and co-chairs, introducing the theme, inviting speakers, organizing a discussion, thanking speakers, introducing the next speaker and closing a session. Appropriate and effective speeches are necessary for a session chairperson to smoothly complete his tasks. The following is an example of a session chairperson's speech.

Sample 1	
Chairing the Plenary Session of the 35th Congress on Peaceful Use of Atomic Energy, May 9 – 11, 2002	
Your excellencies, beloved ladies, gentlemen and friends,[1]	1. Salutation
Good morning! Please allow me now to call the meeting to order. First, **I welcome** you all on behalf of the Executive Committee of the Congress on the Peaceful Use of Atomic Energy. Let me introduce myself. I am Yang Qing from China, serving as chairman for this morning's session. **We are very much honored to** have Dr. Elton Doyle, professor of physics from Indiana University, sitting on my left, as co-chairman with me. Miss Nellie Pierce acts as secretary of the meeting.[2]	2. **Opening the speech, welcoming participants, and introducing chairpersons**

The purpose of this meeting is to exchange experience and knowledge in regard to the theories, new developments and practical applications of two promising techniques of civil engineering. A number of scholars and experts will read academic papers, each of which will take about thirty minutes. It is our hope that there will be half an hour at the end of each meeting left for group discussion.[3]	3. **Introducing the purpose/theme**
The first speaker today is Dr. Soddy, professor of chemistry at the New York University. A native of New Jersey, Professor Soddy holds the BS and MS degrees from Michigan University and the PhD degree from Columbia University. His **major field of interest and professional career** has always been chemical industry or been linked with it. He is an outstanding member of many international professional societies throughout the world. It is really a great pleasure for us to have him address us. His lecture is entitled "Chemistry for Peace". **Now I would like to invite him to deliver his lecture. Let's welcome him with warm applause.** Professor Soddy, please![4]	4. **Introducing the keynote speaker** (educational background, achievements, etc.)
... Compliments: Thank you, Dr. Soddy. I think all the participants present here this morning will agree with me that your **presentation is very informative and enlightening. You address to us about** the new development trends of chemistry and the purpose of it. Yes, the development of chemistry should cater to the needs of all the people and work for the interest of world peace. People who love peace will applaud your valuable advice. **I believe that all of us have benefited a lot from your speech. Thank you.**[5]	5. **Summarizing the major points of the speech**
Now let's welcome our next speaker Prof. Dickens.[6]	6. **Keeping the conference moving**

Exercises

❶ Read the above sample and tell what the chairperson needs to do basically when chairing a group work.

(1)
(2)
(3)
(4)
...

The following are references of sentence patterns and phrases used at different stages by a chairperson.

(1) **To Open a Meeting**
- By self-introduction
  ➢ Ladies and gentlemen, my name is ✽✽✽. I am from Beijing, and I'm going to chair this morning's session. It's a pleasure this morning to welcome you, my colleagues from all over the world, to our conference. Now, I declare the meeting open.
- By the third party's introduction
  ➢ I feel very honored to have been appointed the chairman of this meeting. Thank you, Dr. ✽✽✽. Dear friends, honorable delegates, on the occasion of the opening of this meeting, I would like to express my best wishes for success to this memorable assembly. I would very much appreciate your cooperation and support. Now, shall we start?
- By direct announcement
  ➢ Friends, colleagues! May I have your attention, please? It's time for us to start. Attention, please. Shall we get down to business? The program today will be like this ...

(2) **To Introduce a Speaker**
- By direct introduction
  ➢ I have great pleasure of introducing Professor ✽✽✽. Professor ✽✽✽ comes from Beijing.
  ➢ Ladies and gentlemen, our first speaker is Dr. ✽✽✽. Dr. ✽✽✽ is a distinguished professor from the United States. He is going to talk about the industrial

application of lasers of various types, but he will touch on some of the theoretical aspects as well. Well now, I'll hand the chair to our speaker.

- By appreciative introduction
  ➢ Dr. *** is a figure who is being closely watched by academic circles because of the success of his research. In fact, his achievements are highly esteemed in the world. He will deliver his opening address to the General Assembly. Now, Dr. ***, please.

- By background introduction
  ➢ Now I have the pleasure of introducing Dr. ***. Dr. *** is from Beijing. Last year, I visited his institute and particularly his national key laboratory, and was impressed by his excellent work. Today he will share his new findings with us. Dr. ***, please!

- By transitional introduction
  ➢ Ladies and gentlemen, from the talk of Dr. ***, I believe that every one of us has gained a much better insight into ... in the United States. But what about its application in the development of ... Now, I should like to call upon Professor ***, who would like to make a presentation on his recent survey. Now, Professor ***, please!

(3) **To Organize a Discussion**

- Calling on participants
  ➢ Thank you, Professor ***, for giving us such an enlightening lecture. Hope we all the audience could take advantage of the precious chance to discuss frankly and actively. Now, any questions about Professor ***'s speech? No? But I have a question.
  ➢ Who would like to respond to that point?

- Reminding speakers
  ➢ Could you please make your point more clearly?
  ➢ Well, I'm afraid that we have gone too far from our main theme. Let's come back.
  ➢ Let's keep to the immediate subject, which is ...

- Moderating disputes
  ➢ This is a very meaningful discussion; however, I am afraid we have to stop now or maybe we could continue after the conference due to the time limit.

- Generalizing main points
  ➢ So far we have discussed the following three points: ...
  ➢ The opinions presented so far may be summarized as follows ...

(4) **To Invite Questions from the Audience**
- We have several minutes for questions. If you could, please go to the mike and ask a specific question of one or more of the panelists.
- Okay, I appreciate your attending the session and listening and giving your attention to the speakers. We shared some ideas and thoughts with you. We have tried to share some things that have worked well within the organizations that we worked with. Now, it is time for a dialogue. I would be happy to hear ideas and concepts that you have, as well as questions that you may have. If you would, please step to the microphone and identify yourself and your organization for the record.
- Any questions or comments? If you have, come to the floor microphone, please.
- Now, I think we have just a few minutes for any questions that anyone might have. Who would like to lead off? Okay, we have one. Go ahead.
- I know it's very close to three o'clock, but we're willing to stay until the break time if you guys are willing to do that and especially if you have any questions or comments for any of our three panelists.
- Well, we have such a crowded program, we don't have a lot of time for questions, but we do have some time and I hope we will have some discussion if we can get people from the audience who may want to contribute some of their experiences in (*the construction industry of things that they have noticed that could be done to reduce the risk of ergonomics injuries*). Does anybody want to get up? Any questions?
- Can we get the lights, please? I guess we will open the floor now to questions and answers.
- Well, that is probably a record. (*One ex-university professor and two university professors*) finished 15 minutes ahead of time. There will be 15 minutes for questions for anybody who has questions. I think this afternoon we have said some very different things and some contradictory things. And so, one would hope that there might be some questions.
- We have a few minutes for questions. I would like to invite any questions for Mr. *** first because he is going to have to leave to catch a plane. Is your question for Mr. ***? Would you go to the microphone, please?
- This is an opportunity for any questions, comments, or concerns you may have of the speakers. From the audience? Yes, in the back?
- Okay. Any questions? We have about ten minutes. I would like to kind of go

> over here now, and we will pull together any questions and answers.
> Let's go ahead and open things up to the audience here. That gentleman, do you have a question? Could you direct it to whoever?
> Our allocated time is almost up. Now I would like to answer one more question.
> Any other questions? One more.
> Mr. ***, last quick question.
> One or two more questions. I think you were next.
> Any additional questions? Let's take this as the last question.

(5) To Invite the Presenter to Answer

> Either of you want to comment on that?
> (Chico), did you have a comment?
> Do any of you want to comment on that?
> (Bill or Robert), would you like to comment?
> Any other quick comments on those two questions, or should we proceed to the next one?
> Let's get comments from any of you on those. (Ron), do you want to start?
> Any other comment on tat? (Mark), you might want to comment on (the American side) on (the political question).
> Anybody?
> Any other final comments?
> Does anyone else want to respond to (Susan's first part about the ad)?

(6) To Close a Meeting

> I thought I'd now summarize briefly what has been said so far ... Our time is up. So let us cut off our discussion at this point for the time being.
> Any additional questions from the floor? If so, please ask. Hearing no question and not seeing anybody at a mike, I'd like to thank the panel and suggest we give them a round of appreciation.
> Okay, well, thank you all for your attention and your time. I appreciate it very much. I am sorry to say that this session will have to stop here. Thank you for your illuminating questions. I would be very glad to discuss them with you after the meeting.
> With that, I would like to close the session by thanking the speakers, (*** of Lowes Company, *** of J. C. Penney, and ***, Jr. of Murphy Warehouse).
> Thanks a lot. Why don't we conclude this session? Thanks for your patience

in allowing us to run a few minutes over. Certainly, if you have any questions, the presenters are still here and there are also papers that were left on the registration table. Thank you.

➢ I think I've got to draw this session to a close. But before I draw it to a close, I've got to thank (*** *from NIOSH*) for putting this session together and getting us all to come to talk. (*Again, thank you very much, Jim.*) And thank you all for coming.

➢ Any other questions? Well, we do appreciate your patience and willingness to share with us your experiences as well. I hope that you enjoy the rest of the afternoon. Drive safely or fly safely.

➢ Thanks a lot for coming and have a good lunch.

➢ Well, thank you very much. I hope this was as good a session for you as it was for us. If you have any questions, we will be up here for a few minutes right now before lunch.

➢ Additional questions from anyone in the audience? If not, on behalf of the three of us, we greatly appreciated all of your interaction with us.

Chapter 4

Making Presentations

Academic presentation is a structured, prepared and speech-based means of communicating information, ideas or arguments to the audience. It is an opportunity to showcase research findings, propagate new ideas, outline a plan or project, or recommend solutions to some existing problems. Hence, skills of making presentations in international academic activities are essential to the professional development of scientists and researchers.

This chapter will provide necessary information and practical skills on the following aspects:
- Starting and ending a speech presentation
- Developing a speech presentation
- Reading manuscripts
- Other factors

Section 1
Starting and Ending a Speech Presentation

Warm-up

> Please read the following three paragraphs and tell which of the three is (are) more appropriate for the context of oral presentation.
>
> A. You can see here, 35% of the group of managers classified as participative reached senior management position. On the other hand, 74% of the more individualistic mangers achieved senior management status.
>
> B. An individualistic style appears to be closely associated with rapid career path progression, whereas a group or participative style, despite its evident attractiveness to all members of staff, is correlated with a relatively slow career progression.
>
> C. So, we find there is a massive contradiction. Good managers are supposed to be participative—to make sure they consult and discuss. Good leaders are supposed to be strong individuals—able to make decisions on their own.

Presentations can be made by speech or poster. A poster presentation advertises a project. It combines text and graphics to present the project in a way that is visually interesting and accessible. It allows the presenter to display his work to other scholars and receive feedback from them. The formats of poster presentations vary with conference requirements, but in every case, a poster should clearly articulate what the presenters have done, how they did it, why they did it, and what it has contributed to the research field and to the welfare of the whole society.

Speech presentations, or oral presentations, are kinds of intellectual conversations that combine theories, methods and data for professionals in certain fields. When one delivers a presentation at an academic conference, the audience can only rely on the speaker's speech and PowerPoint to comprehend his research findings and innovative viewpoints. Reading a serious and lengthy research paper word by word to the audience will make the presentation dull and inefficient. Therefore, the speech at an academic conference should not be a complete copy of the research paper.

When making speech presentations, it's essential to learn about the differences between oral English and written English. Oral English is generally personal and informal in style, using short sentences, simple grammar and plain vocabulary. It requires appropriate use of tone, accent, eye contact and body language. Usage of correct persons, relatively short and simple structures, and of some casual expressions will help to make presenters understood better by the audience, and to achieve a better atmosphere for communication. However, written English is generally impersonal and formal in style, with frequent occurrences of longer sentences, complex grammar and professional terms and expressions. Actually, both oral and written styles are embodied in speech presentations due to the purpose of academic exchange.

A speech presentation consists of 3 parts, opening, body and ending. This section deals with opening and ending of a speech presentation.

1. Starting a Speech Presentation

(1) Salutation and Greeting

At the beginning of a speech presentation, the speaker will greet the chairperson and the audience first. Usually, the more important figures, or the elder ones will be greeted first, then the less important or the younger ones.

To different roles of the attendees, different salutations are required. To a king or a queen, "Your Royal Majesty", "Your Majesty", "Your Royal Majesty Queen Elizabeth" or "Your Majesty King Carlos" are appropriate addressing ways. To a royal family member, "Your Imperial/Royal Highness" or "Your Royal Highness the Prince of Wales" are acceptable.

To a head of government, such as the president of a nation or minister of a government department, a speaker should cheer him or her by "Your Excellency", "Your Excellency Mr. President" or "Your Excellency Mr. Premier". When there are many heads of government are present, the speaker should say "Your Excellencies".

To a prominent figure in academic circles, such as a president or an honorary president or a secretary-General of an international academic association, the speaker should address by his/her title, such as "Respected Honorary President Dr. Smith" or "Respected Secretary-General Dr. Cook". To the chairperson of a conference, "Mr. Chairman" or "Ms. Chairwoman" or "Madam Chairwoman" or "Mr. Chairman and Co-chairman" is often used.

Then comes the participants or delegates of the conference, and they can be addressed as "Ladies and Gentlemen", "Distinguished Colleagues", "Fellow Delegates" or "Distinguished Guests from Europe and North America". These verbal expressions are often accompanied by body languages such as bowing, nodding and smiling.

(2) Means to Begin a Presentation

After the salutation and greeting, the speaker begins his presentation. The following means are widely used to begin a presentation.

1) Beginning by straightforwardness

To come straight to the point without any roundabout statement is the most common way to begin a presentation. A speaker can start introducing his or her topic by saying "now I would like to speak about ...", "my topic today is ...", "it's my purpose this morning to report on ...", etc.

A speaker can then introduce the framework of his or her speech by saying "My presentation consists of two parts. One is ... and the other is ..." or "I'll first talk about ... and then touch on ... And finally discuss ..." More examples are as follows:

- ✓ Good morning, Mr. Chairman, ladies and gentlemen. The title of my presentation is ...
- ✓ Good morning, Mr. Chairman, fellow colleagues. First, I'd like to tell you briefly the background of my paper, and then present my three hypotheses.
- ✓ Good morning, what I would like to talk about is mainly ... Now, I'm going to briefly list a number of its basic characteristics. They are ...
- ✓ Good afternoon, ladies and gentlemen. I have been greatly enlightened by the previous talks I have heard here. And now, I would like to talk about my own work, which will be dealt with in the following way ...
- ✓ Good morning, Mr. Chairman, representatives. I am very glad to have the opportunity to report my research on such an occasion. I'll lay my stress on the following three aspects. The first aspect is ...

2) Beginning by appreciation

A speaker can start by expressing thanks. Examples are:

- ✓ First of all, I would like to thank our Mr. Chairman and our generous hosts, for providing so many professionals from all over the world with such a pleasant atmosphere to meet, exchange views, and share thoughts and findings. Good morning, my colleagues. What I like to talk about is ...
- ✓ Thank you, Mr. Chairman. Good morning, ladies and gentlemen. What I am going to say can be roughly summed up into the following three points. First,

let's see PPT No. 1. (*Turning to the computer*) Please!
- ✓ Mr. Chairman, thank you for your warm introduction and also for your efforts in making the opening of the conference so successful. Just now the over-praised introduction you have given me, I think, is meant for the study on "…" that I have been carrying on in recent years. Now I would like to say something about the study, I will welcome your comments at the end …

3) Beginning with background introduction

　　In case the author could not attend the conference due to unexpected occurrences, he might try the following approaches: (i) to call or write to explain to cancel his presentation from the conference agenda; (ii) to call or write to change the oral presentation into poster display; (iii) to ask his team members to present for him. In the 3rd case, namely, the speaker presents the research on behalf of someone else, he would first ask for permission from the chairperson and explain the background to the audience. Examples are:

- ✓ Ladies and gentlemen, Professor *** of Donghu University of Wuhan may be known to not a few present. He's been engaged in the study on artificial intelligence for many years, and a number of his papers have been published. But today he couldn't come for health reasons though he's been invited to attend the conference. At the kind recommendation of our chairman, and as once an assistant of Professor ***, I feel very much honored to be permitted to present the following paper on his behalf. Well, now, in recent yews, Professor *** has been working on …
- ✓ Mr. Chairman, first of all, I would like to make an explanation … The paper I am going to present to you now is mainly finished by Dr. *** from Shanghai Computer Center. It's a pity that he fell ill just before our departure for this conference. Here, on behalf of Dr. ***, I'd like to express our warm congratulations on the successful opening of the conference. The study on frequency standards is the area with which Dr. *** has been occupied …

4) Beginning with wit and humor

　　Speech of humor relaxes both the speaker and the listeners. It can make audience laugh before getting on to the business of the presentation, so it can establish a link between the speaker and the audience. But the joke or humor should be related to the topic, and be elegant or graceful to agree with the formalness and strictness of the academic event.

　　If the subject matter of a humorous remark or punch line is not directly related to the speaker, his topic, or at least his next couple of sentences, the "witty story" would appear to be a mere gimmick. Be careful not to offend others, and do not mention religion sensitive, politics sensitive, race sensitive topics. Examples are as follows:

- ✓ Mr. ***, ladies and gentlemen, at this season of the year when the oriental cherries are in full blossom, I'm certainly very happy to have the opportunity to come to Tokyo to attend this Super Gravity Symposium. It makes me think that as early as in 1923, Professor Einstein, the founder of Relativity, came to visit Japan. He then wrote, in a letter to *** of Denmark, a Nobel prize laureate, that "I am charmed by Japan and the Japanese and am sure that you would be, too." I now guess, everyone might have such a feeling at this moment. In the light of Relativity, we ...

- ✓ Mr. Chairman, ladies and gentlemen, good afternoon. Today I'd like to talk about the MIS in China. But don't be mistaken—the "MIS in China" is not a young lady in China. MIS is a short form for Management Information System. It is an integrated user-machine system for providing information to support operations, management, and decision-making functions in an organization. MIS in China ...

- ✓ Good afternoon, everyone. There is a Chinese saying "with a hare under one's garment" to describe the uneasiness for a nervous person. That is how I am feeling at such a moment, and before such a big audience, there seems to be a hare under my garment. Well, now, speaking about "nervous", I would like to show you the result of my experiment on the nervous system of a rabbit ...

- ✓ Good morning, everyone. Someone says that the Internet is an ocean of information and people who want to find information that accords with their interests are the fishers who want to find fish that have good taste. Since the main topic of the meeting is refutation retrieval on Internet I'm glad to see so many Internet fishers here to share my experience of fishing. My work on the Internet information retrieval is focused on ...

5) Beginning with impromptu and occasional references

Sometimes the prepared opening is blocked by happenings relative to the report, or the situation changes unexpectedly.

In this case, the speaker might produce an unprepared opening according to the context. This can be called as an "impromptu opening", which is closely related to the current atmosphere and easily arouses the interest of the audience. Examples are:

- ✓ In memory of the 100th anniversary of the death of Maxwell (1883 – 1963) and of the birth of Einstein (1879 – 1955), the president of the Academy of

Sciences of the Third World Countries, Professor *** from Pakistan, made the following opening remarks when he received the Nobel Prize.

- ✓ Ladies and gentlemen, the Nobel lectures in physics this year are concerned with a set of ideas relevant to the gauge unification to electromagnetic force with the weak nuclear force. These lectures nearly coincide with the 100th anniversary of the death of Maxwell with whom the first unification of forces (electronic and magnetic) matured and with whom gauge theories originated. They also nearly coincide with the 100th anniversary of the birth of Einstein—the man who gave us the version of an ultimate unification of all forces. The ideas of today started more than 20 years ago, as gleams in several theoretical eyes. They were brought to predictive maturity more than a decade back. And they started to receive experimental confirmation some 6 years ago ...

- ✓ Students, yesterday evening, I went to see a film. When I got there, I found the film had already begun, and there was a stretch of darkness inside the cinema. I felt very perplexed, for my eyesight has been very poor. How could I find my seat? I walked in as I thought. Suddenly, I found something very strange on the back of the first seat along both sides of the middle aisle. I could see a small illuminated plate with a very soft green light, on which the seat number was displayed. Without usher, I found my own seat immediately. I sat there and also found a number of soft given lights (like those behind the seats) from the signs of "Exit", "Toilet", "No Smoking Indoor" and other parts of the theater. After the film was over, I went to take a look at an illuminated seat-number plate, and touched it. It was fairly cool, flat, only as thick as two pieces of glass put together. And I'm sure a small bulb can't be placed inside the cavity, what kind of a new light source is it? Oh. I see, it is ...(*Then the lecturer turned to his topic "Heat-Proof Plain Bulb".*)

The beginning part covers about 10%~15% of the whole presentation speech, so it should be concise and tightly relevant to the speech topic. Apology at the start, which is a common Chinese way to show modesty, is inappropriate here since it may leave an impression on the audience that the research work is not well-prepared and deserves no attention.

Exercises

❶ The following is adapted from a presentation. Please complete it with the right forms of the given words.

| welcome | advance | invite | adopt | view |

I feel honored to have been __(1)__ to speak today at the opening of this Seminar cum Workshop on "Medical Education Reform: Hong Kong Experience". I would also like to add my own warm __(2)__ to those visiting Hong Kong for this event. Sharing with other participants your __(3)__ and experience in __(4)__ problem-based learning in your institutions will no doubt help to __(5)__ the modernization of the medical curriculum for the training of better doctors for tomorrow.

❷ The following is part of a presentation beginning. Please refer to the hints in Chinese and complete it.

（1）(问候，开始自我介绍)_____. My name is Andrew Baxter. Today, (2)(引入主题)_____ the laws of robots. (3)(说明发言分为四部分)_____. First of all, I would like to talk about the state of robotics in China today. (4)(其次)_____, we will look at the use of robotics around the world. (5)(再要讨论)_____, some issues of robot safety in factories. (6)(最后结论)_____ with the future of robotics in China. I'd be glad to (7)(愿意回答问题)_____ at the end of my talk.

2. Ending a Speech Presentation

An ending of a speech presentation accounts for about 6% of the whole speech in length. An effective ending can deepen the audience's impression of the speech. In the ending, the presenter can wind up directly, make a brief summary of his main points, or invite solicitation. The following 3 means are widely used in the ending of a presentation speech:

(1) To End with Direct Wind-Up

✓ That's all. Thank you, Mr. Chairman. Thank you all.

✓ … I think that is all there is to say at present. Thank you, ladies and gentlemen.

✓ … Well, I think this might be a good place for me to wind up my talk. Thank you everyone.

(2) **To End with a Brief Summary**

✓ ... The themes I have dealt with can be boiled down as follows: Firstly, the knowledge and wisdom of human beings should be integrated; secondly, the new information technologies should be adopted; thirdly, the computer-based models should be established; and last but not the least, the study of system science, methodology and methods of systems engineering should be carried out comprehensively. That's all for my talk. Thank you for your attention.

✓ ... In case I have made my careless mistakes and in order to clarify what I have said, let me just go over the main points again ... That's all. Thank you, everyone.

(3) **To End with Solicitation of Comments**

✓ ... That's all for my talk. Please don't hesitate to put forward your suggestions and advice. Thank you.

✓ ... That's all for my talk. If there are any points that I didn't make clearly, please point them out and I would like to give further explanations. Thank you.

✓ ... As time is limited, I can just give you the outline of what I've been studying. For any question to be raised, I'm quite willing to discuss them with you at any time after the conference. Thank you.

❸ **Read the following three samples and find out typical expressions or sentence patterns used for presentation beginning and ending.**

Sample 1

Presentation at International Conference on Healthcare Resource Allocation for HIV/AIDS (ICHRA) October 13, 2003

Opening paragraph

It's wonderful. Thank you very much indeed, Jose, and all those who were involved in nominating me. I feel very honored indeed. But I'd like to say that the real heroes are the patients—the people affected by HIV and AIDS, their caregivers, the people who are struggling every day in their own lives with HIV. But thank you very much. Well, I've been asked to speak about care for adults and children with HIV and AIDS. Like Alice, I've had problems in trying to limit my lecture to 15 minutes. It's very difficult to decide exactly what to include and what not this whole field and there is so much that could be said. I'd like to start by just reminding us of the context in which we must look at care. Where is the HIV burden most heavy? I think we all know the answer to that but let's just have a look at where the burden is.

   ...

Ending paragraph

Finally, let us always remember that this epidemic is about individuals. These smiling and confident children that you see here were able to go back to school with good quality of life. Let's always remember that strengthening healthcare systems is all about improving the quality of life for individuals. Thank you.

Sample 2

Presentation Transcript at Playback '96

Opening paragraph

Let me thank the organizers of Playback '96 for the invitation to be here with you at this international panel. Flying in here, which means some 15 hours up in the air, I was wondering why and how we were invited to this glimpse into the future. When you live in a country like Brazil, there are only two ways you can look at the reality around you. You will have to realize that you are either a Third World country, or more positively, that you are a country of the future. We have to live with the idea that we are the ninth economy. On the other hand, the third country in income concentration on the planet. It's not exactly something to be proud of. The fact that all this wealth is concentrated in the hands of a happy few means that you have a majority of your population who are sub-citizens, of which 20% are below the poverty line. Prisons are overcrowded, at one hand. At the other extreme, the affluent population is prisoner in their homes, in permanent fright for their personal security. We know there is a gigantic bridge to cross, in order to enclose all of Brazil's Brazilians in this Brazil of the future. Believe me, we're all working hard on it. But let me tell you how I feel this paradox also affects us. In order to survive, we have to be creative. With little or no resources, we have to do a real lot.

We put up a research study to assure us that we were in the right direction. Since we were going to use one medium to teach another medium, video showing the visual arts, we wanted to know the quality of the reception of this media in the classroom, and since we were going into art education, we wanted to compare the traditional modernistic approach, which thinks of art education as an activity, where children are supposed to have fun while they express themselves, or the new DBAE approach, which thinks of art as a discipline, as something to be taught.

Well, so we did. We were expecting favorable results with our research, but the results we got were even better than we expected. Children were able to learn art more and faster with video than without video. And this was even more so when associated with DBAE. I'm not going to go into the scientific findings of the research, since this is not our topic here, but if you are interested, I can send you material about it. We published a book about it, in Portuguese, of course.

...

Ending paragraph

So, I would like to finish with a proposal. I think we are here at the final moments of Playback '96, which we want to be a landmark, as far as video preservation goes. We will hear what our colleagues have to say, but from my point of view in Brazil, I can feel already that there was a big step taken before this conference, when you had the regional panels throughout the United States. I feel that it's now the moment to go internationally, and to hear what the countries have to say in that matter, and where the solutions come from. Yesterday, we were speaking about what it means to have the multinational companies on one hand, and the needs on the other hand. Why don't we put hands in hands, and try to, together, confront this reality?

Sample 3

Presentation Cyprus 97 by O. V. Usha, Writer from Kerala, India

Opening paragraph

Respected Chairperson,

Professor Stephanides,

Vice-Chancellors,

Friends,

First of all, let me express my sincere gratitude to the Association of Common Wealth Universities for inviting me to this conference. I have been invited as a writer and I consider this invitation a great honor bestowed upon me and upon India to which country I belong. At international gatherings where Indian literature is represented, literatures of the Modern Indian languages seldom get a chance. This recognition of the Indian languages is a very happy turn. Malayalam the language to which I belong as a writer cannot boast of a very long history of literature compared to some of the other languages of India, like the Tamil. Yet Malayalam literature has matured and is now a lively literature that is still growing. The Malayalis have indeed proved their creative genius and contributed to the rich texture of the literatures of contemporary India. Kerala, the home of the Malayali, is placed at the southernmost tip of the Indian peninsula on the coast of the Arabian Sea. Kerala has been a door to India for traders, including East India Company. Christianity came to us in the first century AD earlier than it arrived in Europe. Legend has it that St. Thomas himself baptized the first generation of Christians in Kerala. Islam is the other dominant religion that has taken root. Among older religions, apart from sanskritic Hinduism, Buddhism and Jainism have had their influence on this land. Coming to recent times we have Marxism, modernism and post-modernism influencing us. In addition Keralites go out and bring a bit of culture from wherever they go seeking better opportunities. There is a tremendous inter-mixing of many streams in blood and culture in the Keralites. Yet they manage to remain distinctly Malayali.

> Now I am here against this background and experience joy and humility at the same time in being chosen to make this presentation. The topic I am asked to speak on is "University and Society: A View for Tomorrow". I must confess that I am no scholar and I am merely seeking to share my views as a person caught in the hub of changes brought on by the clash between tradition and modernity. The University could be viewed as an institutionalization of the Western learning process. It has become the global model as an offshoot of Western imperialism and colonialism although these no longer exist in their stark original forms.
>
> ...
>
> **Ending paragraph**
>
> Last but not the least, the spiritual teacher Karunakara Guru has foreseen a new age, the mark of which will be a truly higher learning in which awareness plays the key role. And to conclude I quote the Guru once again: Education should retrieve science from lending itself to unscrupulous ways destructive to mankind.

❹ The following is a presentation ending. Please complete it with the appropriate phrases in the box.

A. such an initiative	B. very successful and fruitful
C. among our eight institutions	D. spread to a wider audience
E. for the greater good	

The sharing of good practices is another area that the University Grants Committee seeks to promote (1) _____. We feel that only through experience-sharing activities can the philosophy and culture of good learning and teaching be (2) _____ and in turn benefit the higher education sector as a whole. This Seminar cum Workshop is an excellent example of (3) _____, bringing institutions in various parts of Asia together to share experiences in medical education reform (4) _____ of the Asian communities.

Once again, I would like to welcome you all here and I wish the organizers and all participants a (5) _____ series of discussions.

❺ Put the following parts of a presentation ending in the right order.

    A. First, because of rationalization, it seems that we will find many reasons not to go on a diet.

    B. Thank you!

    C. In closing, I would like to leave you with my theory on dieting.

    D. Today I have shown you two reasons why people find it difficult to begin and stay on diets.

E. It is almost impossible not to yield to the pressure of friends who need your help.

F. Secondly, we bow to peer pressure.

Section 2
Developing a Speech Presentation

Warm-up

Read the following text and discuss with your partner how it is developed.

Mr. Cook, a renowned American historian, arranges the books on his bookshelves in a unique way. In the upper right-hand corner, there are books about the development of the early colonies in New England and the War of Independence. Right under them can be found books on the slave trade, the plantation system and the growth of the southern states. The left side of the shelf contains hundreds of books concerning subjects of the Westward Movement, Indian Culture, the cowboys' contributions to American society and the Gold Rush in California. From the description above, one can see that Mr. Cook regards his bookshelves as a map of the U. S. and arranges his history books accordingly. It is odd, but it is convenient.

Developing a speech presentation means to develop a text logically. A text consists of a group of related sentences/paragraphs that are organized in a systematic way to develop one main idea. In academic speech presentations, various developing ways are applied, among which the following are the most frequently used.

1. By Arrangement of Subjects

In paper presentation or thesis defending, speakers normally present their researches by order of subjects, which is similar to the order of subjects in written research articles, however focuses more on description of the experiment or the case. A popular structure of academic presentation is IMRD (Introduction, Method, Results and Discussion). However, different research issues may select different presentation ways. For example, in describing the principles of a certain technique, the speech structure could be: first the definition and application, then the major components, and finally the working principles or processes. In general, subjects of academic speech presentations cover all or some of the following elements: research significance and purpose, theoretical basis, methodology, experiment procedure, result, discussion and analysis, summary and limitations. Examples are:

> ✓ Ladies and gentlemen, it's a great pleasure for me to be able to attend the conference. My topic today is ... First, I'd like to introduce the research background. Then I will explain my experiment. Finally, I will talk about the findings and conclusion.

> ✓ Thank you very much, Professor Smith, for your kind introduction. Mr. Chairman, ladies and gentlemen, good morning. I think it a great honor to be asked to speak about ... in this session of the symposium. My speech covers four parts. The first part deals with the research purpose. The second part discusses the theoretical basis and methodology. The third part presents the experiment procedure and result. The last part is findings and conclusion.

By the above approach to develop a speech, the speaker usually includes in the speech the words and phrases like:

> first, then, finally, at last
> first part, second part, third part
> research background, theoretical foundation, methodology, experiment subjects/procedure/result/findings, conclusion

2. By Chronological Sequence

To develop a speech by chronological sequence will not only give the audience a logical framework of the research, but also enable them to learn about the research work easily.

A chronological pattern is often selected when a speaker intends to emphasize a research issue development or evolution track. Examples are:

> ✓ Well, speaking of the entire-tower lifting, we must, in advance of the lifting, link first the stiffener and the connector of the tower footing with the shoes, and fix them by bolts. These bolts are made of high-strength steel, and must not be replaced by others of ordinary steel.
> During the lifting, we have specially designed a difference in the height for the two tower footings for the good of easy deflection ...

> When the tower body is being lifted about one meter high above the ground, and all sling forces have been exerted, we have a vibration check at this point ...
> As the last step, the beating of the tower will be finally adjusted, the cross-arm will be correctly orientated, the permanent guys will be appropriately mounted, and all the machines and tools will clearly be dismantled and carefully carried away.

✓ > Once you encounter a person who has stopped breathing, you should begin immediately to do mouth-to-mouth breathing. First, place the victim on his back and remove any foreign matter from his mouth with your fingers. Then tilt his head backwards, so that his chin is pointing up. Next, pull his mouth open and his jaw forward, pinch his nostrils shut to prevent the air which you blow into his mouth from escaping through his nose. Then place your mouth tightly over the victim's. Blow into his mouth until you see his chest rise. Then turn your head to the side and listen for the outrush of air which indicates an air exchange. Repeat the process ...

By the chronological sequence to develop a speech, the speaker usually includes in the speech the words and phrases like:

> formerly, previously, meanwhile, afterwards, when, after, until
> first, then, next, finally
> in the early 2010s, in 2011, at the time it was constructed, since 1999, in the last 3 months, at the beginning of this month, now, at present, in advance of, during, when ...
> is being ..., as the last step

3. By Spatial Relation

Another effective approach is to develop a topic according to spatial relationship, which is usually adopted in scientific presentation to describe the position, structure, and three-dimensional relationship of objects.

Based on the spatial (or geographical) sequence, the presentation arranges the major points of a speech in terms of their physical proximity/nearness to or direction from each other. Examples are:

✓ > Various parts are schematically shown here; look, on the top of the cryostat, A, B and C are filling tubes for tanks M, P and R; below the stainless steel jacket with an 8-inch conflate flange, a rotary motion manipulator is rested to control the linear movement. In the middle of the body, there are two butterfly valves connecting tanks P and R. In our setup, the sample temperature can be raised slowly and in a controlled way by adjusting the current in the low-temperature heater H. The heater is fastened at the bottom of the cryostat. Look here, behind the manipulator, we can see 3 spacers with ceramic inserts for electrical leads running to the sample area ...

> ✓ This is the relaxation spectrum of the proton $C_6H_5CH_2CH_3$. To facilitate our illustration, I only say a few words about the first line, the middle line, and the last line on this spectrum.
>
> For the first line, the peak in the middle is the quartet peak of CH_2, the left one is the single peak of C_6H_5, while the right one is the triplet peak of CH_3 and the TMS peak at the extremely right side. As to the middle line, the peak of CH_2 is nearly zero, the single peak of C_6H_5 on the left side is approximately reduced to half of that at the first line; on the right side, we can see clearly the triplet peak of CH_3, which is in phase version. Talking of the last line, the quartet peak at the middle is in reversal phase and slightly longer than that at the first line. And this is the same case with the left C_6H_5 peak. The CH_3 triplet peak on the right side is still higher than the CH_3 peak at the first line.

By the spatial sequence to develop a speech, the speaker usually includes in the speech the words and phrases like:

> here, there, elsewhere
> left, right, front, back
> on one side, behind, beyond, beside, under, above, inside of, outside of, on the top of, at the bottom of, in front of, at the back of

4. From Abstract to Concrete

In academic speeches, some professional terms are abstract and hard to comprehend. To achieve a smooth exchange between the speaker and the audience, an abstract concept or terms is often followed with concrete examples or illustrations. Examples are:

> ✓ When a solid gets colder, it decreases in volume. This is the property of solids. We can make use of the fact that solids expand when they are heated, and decrease in volume when they get colder.
>
> For example, when an iron band has to fit very tightly around a wooden wheel, first we make the iron band a bit smaller than the wooden wheel, then heat the band and make it go on the wheel easily. When it gets colder, it decreases in volume and holds the wheel very tightly …

> ✓ This building recognizes complexities and contradictions. It is both complex and simple, open and closed, big and small; some of its elements are good on one level and bad on another; its order accommodates the generic elements of the house in general, and the circumstantial elements of a house in particular. It achieves the difficult unity of a medium number of diverse parts rather than the easy unity of few or many motional parts.

Words and patterns often used include:

> for example, for instance, common examples are ..., typical examples ... such as ..., that is ..., a concrete example will be ..., the following facts have proved ..., detailed information is given ..., to be more exact ...

5. From Concrete to Abstract

This way is opposite to the previous one. The speaker provides the supporting materials first, and then generalize and draw a conclusion. For example:

> ✓ Whether you do or do not open a gift in the presence of the giver; whether you should or should not turn the plate over to look at the maker's symbol on the back; whether you put your coat on before or after you leave the host's house; whether you eat as quietly or noisily as possible; whether you carry on a conversation during a meal; whether you walk in front of or behind a seated person; whether it is a friendly or offensive gesture to put your hand on the arm of the person with whom you are talking—these and a thousand other questions are matters of cultural definition. None of them is inherently right or wrong, and none is good or bad manners except as a society defines it so.

Words and patterns often used include:

> boil down to ..., sum up, put it into a nutshell, in the final analysis, all in all, the above facts have proved that ..., from that we can see ..., in conclusion, as a result, consequently, therefore, thus

Exercises

❶ **Read the following paper presentation at a conference and then answer the questions below.**

(1) Who is the presenter?

(2) What's the title of the presentation?

(3) On what study is the presentation based?

(4) Where was the study conducted?

(5) Could most of the Asian parents provide their kids with regular assistance in learning? Among whom might the situation that the students and their parents were facing be common?

Sample 1 Mr. Chairman, Ladies and gentlemen,	Salutation
My name is Xiwu Feng, from LaGuardia Community College. I am presenting with Mrs. Heping Li, teacher from John Bowne High School in Queens. **The topic** we will discuss is Parental Involvement and Student Achievement—Perceptions and Challenges of Asian Parents and Students. **This presentation is based on our recent study of** parental involvements by Asian parents and their children's academic performances in a New York City public school district. **The examination of student achievement indicates that** there was a high correlation between students' performance and parents' involvement. **The results of the survey show** some interesting findings on perceptions of the Asian parents towards their children's learning and perceptions of the students toward their parents' involvement in their learning. **We would also like to reveal** some concerns and challenges that Asian parents face in helping their children's learning.	Self-introduction Topic Brief introduction to the study content and results
Research has shown that more frequent parental involvement results in students' higher achievement. The parents we worked with also recognize that. **Now I'm going to talk about the results of the study by showing some of the data collected through analyzing the data**, we are able to see how these parents feel about their involvement in their children's learning and what they actually do in supporting their children's learning.	Data analysis
Ⅰ. **Parental Involvement** In response to the question on the frequency of parents helping students, 11% of the parents helped students daily while 18% helped once or twice a week. That means half of the parents couldn't provide their kids with regular assistance in their learning. Ⅱ. **Students' Perceptions** Now I would like to show how students perceive parental involvement with their personal experiences. These were the students who were taking social studies and whose parents participated in the parental involvement survey. Student survey was conducted through an informal inventory. Similar questions were asked and students' responses were interesting. The following are the questions and students' responses:	Details about data analysis

... We found out that students' responses were consistent with those by their parents to some extent.	
Our survey was conducted in a local area and its results may not be appropriate for generalization. Yet the situation the students and their parents were facing might be common among the new immigrant families. Many of them settled down in their little community as they arrived. They are pretty much isolated from outside, speaking their native language, eating the same food, shopping in the convenient stores, watching the TV programs in their native language. They never have the chance to improve their English. As a matter of fact, they don't feel the need. The openness and generosity of this great city of New York greets people from all over the world and allows them to remain unchanged in their own communities. People are enjoying the convenience and the protection from their little community and begin to forget their original dreams. Of course, many Asian parents who have dreams put on their children, feel desperate when finding themselves helpless in realizing their children's dreams. This is not just a language issue. It is a cultural, social and educational issue considering the younger generations. Educators have the responsibility to teach youngsters knowledge, skills and ability. **Our goal is to help them to learn effectively.** We know effective learning can be realized with all the efforts, including that of parents. Without parents' active involvement in the learning process, students will not be able to see a full success in academy. **Let's welcome parents to this learning project and teach them how to help their children to succeed in learning.**	Limitation Significance

Research goal

Implication |
| Thank you. | Expressing thanks |

❷ **Read Samples 1 and 2. Tell if they are similar or different in the style, and then describe the similarities and differences.**

Sample 2	
Mr. Chairman,	
Dear Colleagues,	**Salutation**
Ladies and gentlemen,	
It's a pleasure for me to be here today. Now I would like **to focus on** the cultural significance of silence in the classroom.	**Expressing honors; introducing the topic**
The first thing I would like to talk about is the notion of silence, of being shy, because a lot of people say they are shy. That is used as a common term to describe that these people are shy. They are just faces in a crowd. They don't talk. They're voiceless. But, that's just a common term. There are different reasons for being quiet. According to James McClusky, there are seven reasons to be quiet. One is their skill deficiency, social introversion, social alienation, ethnic and cultural divergence, unfamiliarity with academic discourse, lacking confidence in subject matter, and communication apprehension. I think that being shy or quiet in the classroom is one of those seven reasons or a combination of the seven reasons, but for most immigrant students it's the ethnic and cultural divergence.	**Point 1**
Well, let's move on to the next point. The silent behaviour, or being quiet or I choose not to talk is a learned behaviour as when researchers said that "an essential part of the acquisition of communication competence is how children learn when not to talk, and what silence means in their speech community". What I want to say is that silence for the Asian, for many students coming from Pacific Asian countries like China, Korea, Japan, is a learned behaviour. In the U.S., when children are growing up, parents talk to babies before they can even talk. They talk to them, and for them, and with them. Kids are encouraged to speak up, "use your words".	**Point 2**

The last point along the lines of exploring the cultural significance is I want to talk about the Confucian notion of hierarchy. The Confucius philosophy emphasizes social and political stability. How do you maintain that social and political stability? You do that through imposing a kind of hierarchy in society, as well as at home. Let me show you an example. This is my childhood, and you can see where we children sit. We sit at lower seats, whereas the grandfathers and fathers or male members of hat generation would sit at the upper seats. Their sides are reserved for female members of the family. So, in a family, we have a hierarchy, so where you sit at the dinner table will show you your status in the family hierarchy. The same is true in society.	**The last point**
There are many other factors contributing to being shy in the classroom. I need to stop here. But if you're interested in getting to know more about how we help students like these, an article by the same title is coming out in the April issue of *Teaching and Leaning: The Journal of Natural Inquiry*.	**Closing; introducing sources**
Thank you.	**Expressing thanks**

❸ **Complete the presentation outline based on the hints in Chinese.**

Beginning	Hello, everyone. (1)（感谢听众）_____ (2)（自我介绍）_____Meng Fanyong and today (3)（引出发言内容）_____ the results of my research report, (4)（说明研究主题）_____ "Employability in China". (5)（指出发言内容与听众有密切关系）_____ as we will soon graduate and either look for jobs or return to jobs.
Stimulation	(6)（说明发言开始前要向听众提问）_____. The question is "How would you rate your employability on a scale of 0 to 100 (100 being the highest level of employability)?" Your answer should consider the following assumptions: Assuming that 50% of the companies in the same industry want to hire you … Later I hope to ask more of you to score your employability. For now, however, let's keep these numbers in mind and (7)（进入正题）_____.

Contents	Let's look at the organization of my presentation. As you can see here, basically, I've divided my presentation into 5 pars. (8)（说明发言开头为研究背景介绍，然后是研究方法、调查问卷结果和结论）_____ _____, possible proposals, and brief conclusion. (9)（说明发言结束后会有简短的提问及讨论）_____ _____. (10) _____ 30 minutes of your time just for the presentation. (11)（接着是）_____ 20 minutes. (12)（说明发言和讨论部分的时间分布）_____ _____. (13)（表示愿意在发言结束后回答听众提问）_____ _____, before moving on to the final interactive 20 minutes sessions. The discussion session will be a very good chance for me to judge my proposals against your reactions, your suggestions and even your own counter-proposals. So, I am especially looking forward to this session.
Background	(14)（首先要介绍有关中国就业体制的背景信息）_____ _____.
Research Methodology	Next, before showing my primary data, (15)（接着简要介绍研究方法）_____. (16)（说明研究目的）_____ is to understand employee awareness regarding the employment system and employability. I distributed the questionnaire to more than 200 JAL employee from Jan. 24, 2002 to Feb. 14, 2002 by using website, email, and handouts. The demographic information that has been included the following: ...
Question Results	As you can see, most employees feel the lifetime employment system and seniority-based employment system cause the Chinese labor market to be rigid ...
Possible Proposals	(17)（进入发言的第四部分）_____ _____. The first proposal is to introduce a flexible year-round recruitment system. (18)（第二项提议为）_____ to introduce incentive development program year-round for competence in specific business fields, including leadership and others. The third proposal is to introduce a merit system.

Conclusion	Because of the nature of the Japanese employment system, employability in China has been quite low. However, the employees and the employer should think more about higher employability from now on. Otherwise, Chinese companies will not be able to win in the competitive market

❹ **Make a paper presentation to the classmates according to the information given below and with reference to the useful expressions and sentence patterns in the textbook. The presentation should include an introduction, a body and a conclusion.**

Topic	A SWOT analysis of the company *NOTE: SWOT stands for strengths, weaknesses, opportunities and threats.*
Main parts	1. Strengths: (1) product page; (2) after-sales team 2. Opportunities: (1) increase sales by 50% – 60%; (2) extend customer base 3. Weakness: Marketing 4. Threat: STERLING (the competitor)

❺ **Select a research paper from the library or online academic databases, read it carefully and then present it to your class. Try to use the following useful expressions and sentence patterns.**

(1) **Declaring the Topic**

➢ In this presentation, I shall confine myself to (*the major points, which appealed to those participating in the Working Groups on Information and Communication Technologies*).

➢ Today I would like to present a brief summary of ...

➢ Today I would like to talk to you about some of our work in the field of ...

➢ What I would like to do today is to review the present situation of ...

➢ My purpose today is to make a general comment on recent progress made in the field of ...

➢ It's my intention to summarize some recent advances in the field of ...

➢ The presentation will address two of the recognized "potential problems" (*for The Immigrant Tourist Industry*): (*the reinforcement of stereotypes about the—"authentic" ethnic or the "authentic" ethnic experience*) and (*the homogenization and fossilization of urban landscapes*).

➢ This presentation will focus on (*ethnic festivals and more mundane spectacles found in Chinatowns which are two genres of commercial precincts or what I have called elsewhere "Ethnic Theme Parks"*).

- I feel privileged to share with you a few thoughts on (*the delivery of education in the context of a knowledge society*).
- It is a pleasure for me to be here this afternoon and to address you on the subject of (*the General Assembly of the WMA held last October in Washington, D. C.*)
- I would like to present (*three propositions about a leadership*) for your consideration.
- I want to talk to you about some preliminary findings of a study I recently conducted.
- I'd like to talk to you about (*the state of robotics in Japan today*).
- I'm delighted and honored to address you this afternoon on the subject (*"Has Humanism Any Future?"*)
- I would like to elaborate on his comments and tie the subject of (*"Governance and Stakeholders"*) to that of (*"Leadership"*).
- I want to talk about (*the immigrant students' use of science and what it means*) and especially to explore (*the cultural significance*), and if I have time I'll quickly talk about (*how as teachers we can help these students in our classrooms*).

(2) **Introducing Major Parts**

- I should like to give this talk in three parts. The first part deals with … The second part concerns … and then the last part relates to …
- Today, I will first discuss … then touch on … and finally describe …
- I would like to make three points with respect to … The first point relates to … Then the second point concerns … The third point is that …
- I think there are two additional points which have to be considered here. One is that … The second point is that …
- I'll lay my stress on the following two aspects.
- I've divided my presentation into five parts: first, I'm going to state the problem; second, give you a framework, state of the art and where things need to be going; third, give you five interesting practices that come from the field that exemplify …
- To address these questions, I'd like to divide my talk into four parts: First, to give you a brief look at (*the word's equity market over the last decade, and Africa's place in it during that time*). Second, to look at (*some of the successes that Africa has achieved*). Third, to look at (*some specific steps that it can undertake to improve its position in the capital markets*). And

fourth, to make some specific recommendations about (*what institutions like the AFDB, multilateral agencies, and non-governmental organizations can do to expedite Africa's capital market development, and accelerate its integration into the global economy*).

➢ My talk is organized into four parts: Part One: (*6 Propositions*); Part Two: (*6 Humanist Beliefs*); Part Three: (*4 Deliberate Omissions*); Part Four: (*Some Practical Pointers*).

➢ I'd like to divide my opening comments into three parts: (*the spiritual message of the Quakers to the current peace movement, a few simple facts, and my thoughts on how we have to proceed*). After this, I will discuss (*some of the work we're doing to support conscientious objectors and those interested in alternatives to military service*).

➢ I will highlight three broad issues that I hope will be useful to you for your discussion today. The first of these is (*how the Structural Funds fit into the UK's regional policy*). The second issue I'd like to discuss is (*the role of the Structural Funds in helping to deliver the improvements I've been talking about*). For my third and final issue, I'd like to turn to (*the debate about the future of the Structural Funds*).

(3) Discussing Points

➢ Now, let's talk about / look at / consider / deal with / go through / discuss ...

➢ The first point I would like to make about ... is that ...

➢ The next point I would like to bring up has to do with ...

➢ Now let's turn to ...

➢ I would like to shift to the topic of ...

➢ Let's move on to the next problem of ...

➢ I'd like to leave the topic of ... and consider / talk about ...

➢ I'll restrict myself to the results of our observation on ...

➢ I would like to confine my discussion to ...

➢ The first of these I want to discuss is ... and I am going to limit my discussion to ...

➢ Let's look at (*drug addiction*) in the first place.

➢ First, let's look at (*the global equity market*).

➢ The first thing I want to talk about is (*the notion of silence, of being shy, because a lot of people say they are shy*).

➢ Now to the second part of my talk: (*What are the successes? And can we*

point to them, for inspiration, and guidance for the future?)
- A second point, that also needs to be stressed, is that (*those who contribute funds to finance higher education expect something in exchange for their contribution*).
- A second, serious problem is (*the spreading of HIV/AIDS in detention centers*).
- The third area of concern is related to (*the growing problem of trafficking in persons, an evil trade mainly aimed at the sexual exploitation of women and children*).
- Another point I would like to make relates to (*the notion of market-driven higher education*).
- The last in my list of challenges has to be (*access to the technologies by learners*).
- It seems to me that there are three levels that we should look at. First, (*there are the immediate participants*).
- Let's consider the four things that are most crucial. First, (*transparency*). Second, (*openness*). Third, (*the rule of law ...*).

(4) Illustrating Points

- I would like to go/enter into some detail on this point/question.
- I would like to elaborate/expand/enlarge/amplify on this matter with some more slides.
- I'd like to deal with this question in more depth.
- I'd like to discuss this point at length.
- I would like to spend some time describing this point in greater detail.
- I would give a short/brief description of ...
- Without going into details, I just want to point out that ...
- Let me just go through the next two points quickly/briefly.
- In the interest of time/brevity, I won't go/enter into details on this point/problem/subject. Time will not permit me to go over all these things.
- My time is running short. So, I will be brief.
- In the interest of time, I am going to omit describing this part of my speech.
- We can discuss this perhaps during the question-answer period.
- I would like to go back / return to the question of ...
- I would like to refer again to ...
- I will return to this point later.
- I will have more to say about that in a few minutes.

- I will provide you with some specific information about that in a few minutes.
- Now, come back to what I was saying a moment ago.
- Now I would like to address myself to the most important aspects of ...
- I shall concentrate/focus my discussion on ...

(5) Turning to Another Point
- So far, I've presented you with six propositions. And now I'd like to present you with (*music humanist beliefs*).
- A couple of points, at least, need to be stressed when we discuss these issues. One has to do with (*the fact that public higher education remains not only tied to the State, but it is an obligation of the state*).
- We have talked here about (*social responsibility*). There are some relevant questions that need to be addressed again.
- Now I'm going to talk about the results of the study by showing some of the data collected.
- This brings me to my third observation of this presentation. It has to do with (*institutional considerations and challenges*).
- That brings me to a second important observation, which is (*a clash between the market driven and the public-driven*).
- I would like to take a few minutes to highlight (*some of the improvements in this bill over preciously proposed health sector legislation*).
- What I'd like to do now is look at (*four of the things I've consciously omitted*).
- Before concluding, I would like to touch on one other (*important change that I believe would enhance this bill*).
- Before concluding I wish to raise a number of questions reflecting (*the Strasboury system*).

(6) Citation and Exemplification
- Theoretical and methodological discussions will be illustrated and supported by (*comparable photographs taken in cities where "Chinatown" has touristic currency*).
- A complete, rigorous proof of this fact can be found in (*"Invitation to Geometry" written by Z. A. Melzak*).
- The evidence in my findings seems to support (*what I call a cross-cultural identity, fueled by a cultural tension*).
- I can even give another example.

> I take (*just one of his figures*) to illustrate my point.
> On a positive note, it seems that (*they are willing to negotiate the two cultures*), at least according to my findings, as evidenced in (*one of the questions that I asked them*).
> (*Frances Cairncross*) in her book, (*The Death of Distance*), postulated (*a set of trends in the new communications environment, which will influence the way we live, work, play and learn*).
> Before dealing briefly with (*the new Washington Declaration on Biological Weapons*), let me quote (*Dr. Randy Smoak, the Chairperson of the WMA Council*).

(7) **Referring to Others' Presentations**
> Several speakers this morning have emphasized (*the fact that HIV/AIDS is a cross-cutting issue*).
> Now, both of the speakers yesterday made very good points. As the bottom line of their presentations, they both were dealing with (*something that is of the concern of all of us, with financing of higher education*).
> The previous speaker covered points I was going to make about (*financing*).
> It's a great honor to be here and especially to listen to some of the seminars. The one with (*David Scott and Juan Tobias*) was truly brilliant, and I hope I can live up to that.

(8) **Drawing a Conclusion**
> To sum up, my conclusion is that …
> In conclusion, I would like to point out …
> That brings me to the end of my presentation.
> Let me conclude my talk with the following comments.
> I would like to conclude with a few general remarks on …
> I would like to close my speech today by saying that …
> Finally, as a summary statement/description, I would like to say that …
> It would be reasonable to conclude that …

(9) **Closing the Presentation**
> Once again, I want to thank you for the privilege and the opportunity of talking to you about this subject. Thank you very much.
> Ladies and gentlemen, it has been great pleasure for me to exchange my views on this complex problem with you. Thank you.
> Thank you very much for the privilege of presenting this paper.

- ➢ I want to thank the audience for their attention. Thank you, Mr. Chairman.
- ➢ Thank you very much for your kind attention.
- ➢ That's all. Thank you.
- ➢ That concludes my presentation. Thank you.
- ➢ That's all for my presentation. Thank you.
- ➢ To end, if you allow me, I would like to congratulate (*someone who is at this table and is of exemplary courage ... Professor Elmandjra*).
- ➢ I would like to end by quoting from (*another Nobel Laureate, not Ilya Prigorgine, but from a recent book by Robert Fogel, an economist at the University of Chicago*).
- ➢ In closing, I want to note that (*our nation's poet-laureate Billy Collins recently reminded us that, "If political protest is urgent, I don't think it needs to wait for an appropriate scene and setting and should be as disruptive as it wants to be."*)
- ➢ I would like to end on a note of caution.
- ➢ My time is running out. I have to stop here. Any questions or comments?
- ➢ This concludes my presentation, and I would be pleased to answer any question you may have.
- ➢ This is only the beginning of my study, it's a preliminary summary, and I hope to uncover more things. Thank you very much.
- ➢ Thank you for your attention. I would be pleased to address your questions at this time.
- ➢ That's all that I want to talk about this afternoon. Please don't hesitate to ask me if you have questions.
- ➢ That concludes my talk. Thank you very much. So, now I am very interested to hear your comments.
- ➢ I need to stop here. But if you're interested in getting to know more about (*how we help students like these*), an article by the same title is coming out in (*the April issue of Teaching and Leaning: The Journal of Natural Inquiry*). Thank you.

Section 3
Reading Manuscripts Smoothly

Warm-up

Read the following formulas and sentences with your partner.
(1) $a \cdot b = c$
(2) $Na_2CO_3 \cdot 10H_2O$
(3) We know that Madame Curie and her husband's long and arduous efforts were finally crowned with great success in July 1898—they discovered a radioactive element, namely polonium.
(4) The circulating water system (CWS) will be a closed-cycle type of cooling system which consists of cooling tower/basin, pump structure and supply/return pipelines.

Making oral presentations in academic conference is challenging for natives, not to mention non-native speakers. To practice reading manuscripts smoothly means a to-be speaker rehearses beforehand before tutors, colleagues or even a mirror. The reading of a manuscript requires consideration of many factors, including formulas reading, Latin abbreviations reading, punctuations reading and so on. This part will give presenters some tips on accurate and fluent presenting.

1. Various Formulas

Formulas reading is a big challenge to most of the presenters, for example, "+" should be pronounced as "plus", "0" as "naught" in Britain English or "zero" in American English, "x^n" as "x to the nth power", "$\sqrt{}$" as "the root of". Hence, researchers need to have a general knowledge of mathematical symbols, chemical symbols and formulas. The following are examples including commonly used symbols and formulas:

$$\left(8 + 6\frac{5}{8} - 3.88 \times 4\right) \div 2\frac{1}{2}$$

It is generally read as: *eight plus six and five-eighths minus three point eighty-eight multiplied by four, all divided by two and a half.*

It might also be read as: *eight plus six and five over eight minus three decimal double eight times four divided by two and one over two.*

$$ar^{n-1} + \sqrt[3]{x} = A + \frac{B}{T} + \frac{T}{\log R}$$

It is read as: *a times r to the n minus one power plus the cube root of x, equals A plus B over T, plus T over logR.*

$$\int_0^{\frac{\pi}{2}} \frac{dx}{1 + \alpha \cos x} + \sum_{r=0}^{n} \left(\frac{n}{r}\right)^2 = \int_{\lambda-0}^{b} f(x) \, dx$$

It can be read simply as: *the integral from zero to pi over two of dx over one plus α times cosine of x, plus the sum from r equals zero to r equals n of the quantity n things taken r at a time squared, equals the integral from zero to b of function of x.*

Another way to read it is: *the integral from zero to pi over two of the quantity dx over one plus α times cosine of x with respect to x, plus the sum from r equals zero to r equals n of the quantity n things taken r at a time squared, equals the integral between the limits x equals 0 and x equals b of the function of x with respect to x.*

$$(a+b)^n = a^n + na^{n-1}b + \frac{n(n-1)}{2}a^{n-2}b^2 \cdots + b^n$$

It can be read as: *the quantity a plus b to the nth power equals a to the nth power, plus n times the quantity a to the n minus one power times b, plus n times n minus one divided by two, times the quantity a to the n minus two power, times b squared down to b to the nth power.*

$$Fe + S \rightarrow FeS$$

It is read as: *F E and S react to give (or: produce/form/yield/release) F E S.*

$$SiO_2 + 2C \rightarrow Si + 2CO$$

It is read as: *S I O two and two C react to give S I and two CO.*

$$2KClO_3 \xrightarrow{MnO_2} 2KCl + 3O_2 \uparrow$$

It can be read as: *two K C L O three, when heated in the presence of a manganese dioxide as a catalyst, forms two K C L and releases three O two.*

It can also be read as: *two potassium chlorates, in the presence of a manganese dioxide catalyst on healing, form two potassium chloride and three oxygen.*

The second reading is based on meaning and it sounds more practical in oral presentation.

$$6NH_4OH + Al_2(SO_4)_3 \longrightarrow 2Al(OH)_3 + 3(NH_4)_2SO_4$$

It can be read as: *six N H four O H, plus A L two open bracket S O four close bracket three times, yield two A L open bracket O H close bracket three times, plus three open bracket N H four close bracket twice S O four.*

However, in oral presentation or in explaining the equation orally, it will be read as: *When ammonium hydroxide is added to a solution of aluminum sulfate, aluminum hydroxide and aluminum sulfate are formed.*

$$CH_4 + 2O_2 \longrightarrow CO_2 + 2H_2O$$

This equation can be read in five different ways:

(1) *C H four and two O two react to give C O two and two H two O.*

(2) *Methane reacts with oxygen to produce carbon dioxide and water.*

(3) *One molecule of methane reacts with two molecules of oxygen to form one molecule of carbon dioxide and two molecules of water.*

(4) *One mole of methane and 2 moles of oxygen react to produce 1 mole of carbon dioxide and 2 moles of water.*

(5) *One mole of C H four plus 2 moles of O two react to produce 1 mole of C O two and 2 moles of H two O.*

$$pV = nRT = \frac{g}{M}RT \ (ideal-gas\ law)$$

It can be read as: *p V equals n R T equals g over M times R T.*

Where: p = pressure, V = volume, n = g/M, R = ideal-gas constant, T = absolute temperature (to C + 273.15℃), g = weight of gas of molecular weight M.

2. Latin Abbreviations

Latin abbreviations are frequently used in scientific papers and should be read correctly, such as "et al" (and others), "etc." (and so on), "e. g." (for example), "i. e." (that is to say), "viz" (namely; that is). Some of the frequently used Latin abbreviations are listed in the following table with their English equivalences:

Latin Word	Abbreviation	English Meaning
circa	ca.	about
et alii, et eliae	et al	and others
et cetera	etc.	and so on
vide infra	v. i.	see below
exempli gratia	e. g.	for example

continued

Latin Word	Abbreviation	English Meaning
ibidem	ibid	in the same place
id est	i. e.	that is to say
idem quod	i. q.	the same as
loca citato	loc. cit	in the place cited
nota bene	N. B. or n. b.	observe carefully; take notice (in writing to begin a note)
opere citato	op. cit	in the work cited above
quod vide	q. v.	which see (to look in another place to find …)
sic		so; thus (in the bracket after the quotation noting that the mistake is from the original text)
vice versa	v. v.	the other way round
vide intra		see above
vide licet	viz	namely; that is
ide supra		look at an earlier place in a book (used for telling a reader where to find more about the subject)

3. Punctuation

In a written paper, punctuation marks are demonstrated by printed symbols which may not cause any misunderstanding, but in reading, the meaning of these printed punctuations may not be expressed so easily by direct reading without certain treatment.

(1) Parentheses/Brackets

1) Parentheses/brackets in written papers usually explain the previous expressions. For example,

In the experiment mentioned above, we examined the material and all the physical quantities (temperature, pressure and specific weight, etc.) were obtained.

It reads: *In the experiment mentioned above, we examined the material, and all the physical quantities including temperature, pressure and specific weight and so on were obtained.*

2) It is advisable to adopt the following transitional phrases to replace the bracket:

- … which include(s) …
- … which are (is) …
- … in which … are (is) shown as …

- *... from which we obtain ...*
- *... that is ...*
- *... including ...*
- *... that means ...*
- *... please see ...*
- *... as indicated in ...*
- *... such as ...*
- *... namely ...*

(2) **Comma**

Comma indicates a short pause. If not indicated clearly enough according to circumstances, it might cause misunderstanding. For example,

The $K = 0$ component, which does not give rise to a current fluctuation, will not influence the band shape.

If the oral pause after the comma is too short and makes the non-restrictive attributive clause sound like a restrictive attributive clause, as "*The $K = 0$ component which does not give rise to a current fluctuation will not influence the hand shape*", the original meaning of the sentence has changed. By reading in this way, the utterance might imply the following:

1) more than one component which has zero value for K;
2) the component which does not influence the band shape includes only the one which does not give rise to a current fluctuation, which leads to ambiguity.

Another example:

... and under that condition, the electrical energy is converted to heat, light or sound.

Although the sentence is clear enough, the short pause between "heat" and "light", if not clearly made, will inevitably make the noun "heat" sound like a verb so as "to heat light or sound".

In the manuscript reading, misunderstandings like that can be avoided by making a relatively longer pause as in the above example or by adding a word "or" between "light" and "sound". That is to say, the whole sentence may be read as:

And under that condition, the electrical energy was converted to heat, (∨ 换气符号) *light or sound.*

(3) **Quotation Marks**

Quotation marks may function as citation, emphasis, negation, particularization, etc. For example,

The resonance is an extra tunneling channel, or "window". In the barrier

tunneling electrons with total energy E + Er will always be able to see the "window", but do not necessarily exit through it.

The first "window" in this sentence contains a special meaning that refers to the tunneling channel. In this case, some explaining expressions might be added to replace it or to make it clearer such as "we might as well call it ...", "... which may as well be called ..." As for the second "window", only a stress on the article "the" before the word is enough and explanation can be omitted due to the previous one.

Thus, the above sentence can be orally presented as—*In the barrier, the resonance is extra tunneling channel, which may be called a "window". Tunneling electrons with total energy E plus E sub r will always be able to see the "window", but do not necessarily exit through it.*

In order to avoid unclear representation by the pronoun "it", "in the barrier" is here moved to the beginning of the sentence. For example,

The "head-to-foot" erection they began to practice in the early 70's has now been adopted worldwide.

"Head-to-foot" erection is specially used referring to a kind of installation method. In manuscript reading, the addition of the phrase "so-called" before the quoted words might convey the meaning more effectively:

The so-called "head-to-foot" erection they began to practice in the early 70's has now been adopted worldwide.

(4) Dash

A dash is usually a double hyphen. In a text, supplementation or explanation of what is mentioned always follows a dash. A dash is similar in its function to the comma and the colon. A pair of dashes function like a pair of parentheses. Therefore, the way to read a dash, to some extent, is to follow the rules to deal with parentheses. For example,

In the context of discussing properties of solution of differential equations, the scattering wave function should not be given in closed form. Its definition—a particular solution of Schrödinger's differential equation—then is the optimal form.

In reading, the dash in the sentence could be replaced by a relative clause led by "which". "... Its definition, which is a particular solution of Schrödinger's differential equation, then is the optimal form." For example,

We know that Madame Curie and her husband's long and arduous efforts were finally crowned with great success in July 1898—they discovered a radioactive element, namely polonium.

The above example could be read with the dash replaced by "that is" or "namely":

We know that Madame Curie and her husband's long and arduous efforts were finally crowned with great success in July 1898, that is, they discovered a radioactive element, namely polonium.

(5) **Dot**

Dots in scientific writing vary in functions and consequently difficulty arises in the ways of reading.

A dot representing the sign "×" can be read directly as "multiplied by" or "times". For example, "a · b = c" reads "a multiplied by b equals c", or, "a times b equals c".

A dot in a chemistry molecular formula can be read as "dot". For example, the formula $Na_2CO_3 \cdot 10H_2O$ can be read as "N A two C O three dot ten H two O".

(6) **Slant**

The sign "/" referring to alternatives in writing generally means "and", "or", or "and/or". For example,

The circulating water system (CWS) will be a closed-cycle type of cooling system which consists of cooling tower/basin, pump structure and supply/return pipelines.

It generally reads as:

The circulating water system, which is abbreviated as CWS, will be a closed-cycle type of cooling system which consists of cooling tower and basin, pump structure and supply or return pipelines.

The slant will not be read out if put between "and" and "or". For example,

As discussed in Ref. 7, the second term on the right of the above equation represents errors and/or ambiguities in the result of the measurement, while the third term represents the distortion of the state of the system (which is also associated with possible errors and/or ambiguities).

4. Other Aspects

Besides the above three issues, voice, tone, rhythm and posture are also important in oral presentation. Change in sound, such as pauses, being fast or slow, can function to stress or supplement.

A speaker can divide a sentence into meaning groups, pause between meaning groups and read some meaning groups emphatically according to his purpose. Breathe slowly and deeply during the speech. Don't speak too rapidly, which may leave an impression that the presenter is nervous and wants to finish and escape immediately.

In rehearsal, a speaker should avoid using jargons and try to replace jargons with simple words in daily life, such as vomiting instead of emesis. If a piece of jargon is used, the speaker might continue with a sentence or a phrase to explain. It is the same with acronyms (abbreviations). An acronym is a word composed of the first letters of the words. For example, SFG, which stands for Systemic Functional Grammar, is an acronym. When an acronym is used for the first time, the speaker should give its full name.

Remove lexical and syntactic ambiguity and use simple language to present. Due to the nature of oral communication, long, involved sentences often sound obscure and are not preferred though they are sometimes used. Break long, complex sentences into simple, short ones when necessary. Use the active voice and use simple action verbs rather than long phrases.

Imagine the conference hall, the platform, the audience's reaction and possible questions, and get prepared beforehand. Keep relaxed and release the tension in jaw, arms, neck, legs and other parts of the body. Use helpful gestures or movements to divert the nervous energy. Smile is always a good choice.

Exercises

❶ **Work with your partner and read aloud the following sentences to each other. Pay special attention to the reading of abbreviations.**

(1) Present study confirms the suggestion of such a phenomenon by Miller **et al** and is consistent with the two-level collective-emission model.

(2) To treat this singularity, **e. g.** the subtraction method can be used.

(3) It can then be identified with a vector field on the manifold of X, **i. e.** a cross section of the tangent bundle T(X). (**ibid**)

❷ **Work with your partner. Read aloud the following formulae to each other.**

$$\left(8 + 6\frac{5}{8} - 3.88 \times 4\right) \div 2\frac{1}{2}$$

$$ar^{n-1} + \sqrt[3]{x} = A + \frac{B}{T} + \frac{T}{\log R}$$

$$\int_0^{\frac{n}{2}} \frac{dx}{1 + \alpha\cos x} + \sum_{r=0}^{n} \left(\frac{n}{r}\right)^2 = \int_{\lambda-0}^{b} f(x)\,dx$$

$$(a + b)^n = a^n + na^{n-1}b + \frac{n(n-1)}{2}a^{n-2}b^2 \cdots + b^n$$

$$6NH_4OH + Al_2(SO_4)_3 \longrightarrow 2Al(OH)_3 + 3(NH_4)_2SO_4$$

$$pV = nRT = \frac{g}{M}RT\,(ideal-gas\ law)$$

❸ Watch academic presentations of your discipline and imitate the native speakers' presentations in terms of the pronunciation, the tone, the speech rhythm and the speed.

Raising and Answering Questions

Warm-up

1. What is the function of the question-answer session in an academic conference?
2. What questions are often raised in the question-answer session?
3. What could the speaker do to deal with the difficult or challenging questions from the audience?

The question-answer session is an important part of an international academic conference. By asking questions, the attendees can understand the topic better, find solutions to some problems and get inspirations for their own research. By answering questions, the speaker can exchange ideas with other colleagues and identify problems with his research. Hence, a smooth and effective exchange in the question-answer session can bring a win-win result to both the attendees and the speaker.

This chapter will provide necessary information and practical skills in the following aspects:

- Raising questions
- Answering questions

Section 1
Raising Questions

An academic presentation is usually followed by a question-answer session (Q-A session), where the participants can raise questions to the speaker. The questions raised tend to be diverse and complex, and may be difficult to answer since the participants have different research interests though in the same field or discipline. Therefore, the speaker should make good preparation beforehand in order to achieve a good exchange with the participants.

On the other hand, the question raisers should also be well-prepared. For example, he should be acquainted with the conference topics, listen attentively to the given lectures, and additionally, he should be familiar with the strategies and tactics on question raising.

1. Question Raising Speech Structure

At a question-answer session, a listener can raise various questions to the speaker. Basically, the short speech of question raising includes 3 parts: (1) salutation, self-introduction and appreciation; (2) questions; (3) conclusion.

Salutation and self-introduction are formal, polite and brief. Title is to be added when addressing the speaker, e.g. "Professor Jack Smith", "Dr. Liu", "Mr. Li". The self-introduction is a very brief description of the question raiser's name, work or schools and it is often followed with a positive comment on the speaker's speech or a sincere appreciation of the speaker's lecture, e.g. "I am Zhang san from ABC University. Thank you for your vivid and informative lecture.", "I do benefit a lot from your proposed English teaching tactics."

Conclusion symbolizes the end of the question raiser's speech. It's formal, brief and polite, just as the salutation and greeting part. Expressions like "That's all for my question. Thank you in advance.", "That's my personal opinion. Thanks a lot for your consideration." will do.

Questions make up the main part of the short speech, and are illustrated in more details in the following part.

2. Various Questions Raised

In the question-answer session, various questions are asked. For instance, a listener is not sure whether his perception of a point in the speech is correct, or whether he has heard a point clearly, and then asks for confirmation and verification. Generally, questions raised can be divided into four kinds:

(1) **Questions for Problem Clarification**
- ✓ Prof. ***, I don't quite understand what you really mean by saying "…". Can you explain it again?
- ✓ Mr. ***, I would like to ask you a question, or rather, make a request. Is it possible for you to show me again your last slide?

(2) **Questions for Showing Special Interest**
- ✓ Thank you very much for your patient explanation in response to my question. But I have one more question, or rather a request—can I have a copy of your report on the gyroscope? I'm interested in its industrial applications.

(3) **Questions for Raising Different Opinions**
- ✓ Prof. ***, perhaps we're looking at the problem from different viewpoints. To the best of my knowledge, what you say seems to be theoretically unclear in … For example, … Could you give us further explanation on that aspect?
- ✓ Prof. ***, I'm very interested in your presentation on the positive analysis of efficient market hypothesis. But to the best of my knowledge, your viewpoint that … seems to be unreasonable. I'm afraid that … (audience's opinion) Could you give us further explanation on that aspect?

(4) **Questions for Information-Hunting**
- ✓ Prof. ***, I'm very much interested in your presentation today since the work we are going to start is related with yours. Now, would you please say a few more words about the tentative assumption? Particularly at its preliminary stage?
- ✓ Prof. ***, I'm very keen on what you say about the distance from the highest place to the lowest place on the earth. How is it being carried out in your laboratory?

Occasionally the questioners might be arrogant or unreasonable, or might be nitpicking or might go beyond the field of academic discussion. Examples are:
- ✓ Prof. ***, since many companies including IBM and Microsoft are developing new versions of data conference tools, don't you think what

you have done is completely useless?

✓ *You have pointed out that English pervaded through the Internet. Did you think that because of the Chinese language, China could not play an important role in the network?*

It seems that all the questions are asked in a similar way, but in fact, the style of the question raising speeches varies from the question and from the speaker. Usually, the question raiser tends to be more polite in language when the speaker is senior in age or qualification. Besides, when showing disagreement of or doubt on the speaker's viewpoint, the question raiser is supposed to be more polite and euphemistic in language, which will help to create a more friendly atmosphere between the speaker and the questioner.

Exercises

❶ **Refer to the expressions in the textbook and translate the following into English.**

(1) 我是来自北京大学的助理研究员 Jimmy Jin。首先非常感谢你们的精彩展示,我有两个问题:一个是给 Jack Smith 教授的,另一个是给 Michael Green 博士的。

_____

(2) 我对您提到的新算法非常感兴趣,您能就它的实验过程和实验环境多讲一下吗?

_____

(3) Smith 教授您好,谢谢您的演讲。您提到"所有的现象都是相互关联的",我不太理解,您能再解释一下吗?

_____

(4) 请问你们学院近 5 年有多少国家自然科学基金项目?

_____

(5) 如果我没弄错的话,您说压缩率越高,视频质量就越高。但据我所知,一般情况下,视频质量和压缩率应该成反比。您能就此给我们解释一下吗?

_____

_____

(6) 非常感谢您对我问题的耐心解答。我还有一个问题,或者说是一个请求,我能复制您的报告吗? 我对陀螺仪的工业应用非常感兴趣。

_____

_____

❷ **Please read the following 2 presentation lectures and then raise at least 3 questions to each lecture.**

Lecture 1

Mr. Chairman,

Ladies and gentlemen,

My name is Xiwu Feng, from LaGuardia Community College. I am presenting with Mrs. Heping Li, teacher from John Bowne High School in Queens. **The topic we will discuss is** Parental Involvement and Student Achievement—Perceptions and Challenges of Asian Parents and Students. **This presentation is based on our recent study of** parental involvements by Asian parents and their children's academic performances in a New York City public school district. **The examination of student achievement indicates that** there was a high correlation between student performance and parental involvement. **The results of the survey show** some interesting findings on perceptions of the Asian parents towards their children's learning and perceptions of the students toward their parents' involvement in their learning. **We would also like to reveal** some concerns and challenges that Asian parents face in helping their children's learning.

Research has shown that more frequent parental involvement results in students' higher achievement. The parents we worked with also recognize that.

Now I'm going to talk about the results of the study by showing some of the data collected … Through analyzing the data, we are able to see how these parents feel about their involvement in their children's learning and what they actually do in supporting their children's learning.

I. **Parental Involvement**

In response to the question on the frequency of parents helping students, 11% of the parents helped students daily while 18% helped once or twice a week. That means half of the parents couldn't provide their kids with regular assistance in their learning.

II. **Students' Perceptions**

Now I would like to show how students perceive parental involvement with their personal experiences. These were the students who were taking social studies and whose parents participated in the parental involvement survey. Student survey was conducted through an informal inventory. Similar questions were asked and students' responses were interesting. The following are the questions and students' responses:

...

We found out that students' responses were consistent with those by their parents to some extent.

Our survey was conducted in a local area and its results may not be appropriate for generalization. Yet the situation the students and their parents were facing might be common among the new immigrant families. Many of them settled down in their little community as they arrived. They are pretty much isolated from outside, speaking their native language, eating the same food, shopping in the convenient stores, watching the TV programs in their native language. They never have the chance to improve their English. As a matter of fact, they don't feel the need. The openness and generosity of this great city of New York greets people from all over the world and allows them to remain unchanged in their own communities. People are enjoying the convenience and the protection from their little community and begin to forget their original dreams. Of course, many Asian parents who have dreams put on their children, feel desperate when finding themselves helpless in realizing their children's dreams. This is not just a language issue. It is a cultural, social and educational issue considering the younger generations. Educators have the responsibility to teach youngsters knowledge, skills and ability. **Our goal is to help them learn effectively.** We know effective learning can be realized with all the efforts, including that of parents. Without parents' active involvement in the learning process, students will not be able to see a full success in academy. **Let's welcome parents to this learning project and teach them how to help their children succeed in learning.**

Thank you.

Lecture 2

Mr. Chairman,

Your Excellencies,

Ladies and gentlemen,

Several speakers this morning have emphasized the fact that HIV/AIDS is an issuethat cuts across many others. Indeed, the past two decades have shown that drugs crime, the trafficking of human beings, even armed conflicts are important contributors to the AIDS pandemic.

Let us look at drug addictions **in the first place**. Many addicts use contaminated needles and syringes, or have sex under intoxication. As a result, in several Asian countries more than 50%, even 80% of all injecting drug users live with HV/AIDS. Furthermore, more than two thirds of new HIV cases are due to drug injection.

In many countries outside Asia the HIV/AIDS epidemic started with drug addicts and then it spread to the general population. Asia, with its population of 8 million drug injection users faces this risk today. The epidemic can be stopped if drug users are provided with drug dependence treatment, and anti-retroviral therapy. Today, in Asia only five per cent, and in many high-risk areas less than one per cent of all drug users have access to prevention and care services. I urge you all to take adequate measures.

A second, serious problem is the spreading of HIV/AIDS in detention centers. Worldwide, at any given time, there are 10 million prison inmates with an annual turnover of 30 million, many of them being drug users. In many countries prisons are also an HIV breeding ground because of overcrowding, homosexuality, violence, tattooing and the sharing of injection equipment—the United Nations asks all countries to comply with internationally agreed standards and norms of prison management, because of the dignity of human beings under detention but also to avoid the spreading of the pandemic within, and beyond the detention walls.

The third area of concern is related to the growing problem of trafficking in persons, an evil trade mainly aimed at the sexual exploitation of women and children. There are several million slaves under such modern bondage, their number increasing by much as one million per year. Their protection is our collective responsibility: they are human creatures like all of us, at an extremely high risk of HIV infection.

To conclude, Mr. Chairman, the spreading of HIV/AIDS among drug users, among prisoners and among trafficked people is a serious threat. The political, social and health environment need to address this threat or Asia will be robbed of its economic ad developmental successes. UNODC and its partners will continue to assist you all in meeting the endeavor.

 Thank you for your attention.

Section 2
Answering Questions

Similar to the structure of question raising speeches, the question answering speech also includes 3 parts: lead-in, the answer to questions, the conclusion. Lead-in is a brief opening, which includes greeting to the question raiser, expressing appreciation and confirming the correctness of the raised questions with the question raiser. For instance, "Thank you very much for your attention, Dr. ∗∗∗. Two questions are raised, one is …, the other is …, am I right?" It's essential to have a lead-in part before answering the questions, which shows respect to the question raiser on one hand, and confirms the correctness of the questions with the raiser on the other hand so as to avoid the disagreement between the questions and answers. By the way, it's a formal and polite approach to address the question raiser by his title. The conclusion part symbolizes the end of the answer, which usually includes a brief summary of the key points and closing expressions. For instance, "I think that's basically all I can say", or "I hope this answered your question."

To different types of questions, the answers are made differently.

- ✓ **For simple and ordinary questions**, namely, the questions to clarify problems or to show special interest, the speaker can answer briefly and directly. For example, "To answer this question, I'd like to repeat the 3rd point of what I said just now. Well, I was saying …"

- ✓ **For questions of disagreement**, the speaker needs to explain in great detail where the distinction lies in. For example, the speaker could answer, "Well, judging from your question, I can see that your understanding of my viewpoints seems to be somewhat different from my original intention. That awkwardness was due to such short time that I couldn't put it clearly. Here I'd like to explain it briefly. My original intention is …". The speaker could also answer, "I'm afraid that our different views on the point may come from the different angles from which we're looking at the problem. My idea is mainly out of the theoretical considerations, specifically, on the basis of the following three aspects: the first point is …"

✓ **For questions of noncommitment or confidential information** that the question raiser asks for, the speaker may ask somebody else to answer, or answer in a general way, or distract the topic to something else. For example, to a question that the speaker is not familiar with, he may answer, "Fortunately, Professor Smith is here. He has much experience in this experiment. I think no one is more suitable than him to answer your question. / Professor Smith perhaps is in a better position to tell us something about it." To a question that involves some confidential information, the speaker may answer, "Thank you for your question. In your question, you asked me about the number of the ground stations that have been established in my country. I'm very glad to know that you're interested in that. There's no doubt that we've established a number of stations, and with the development of science and technology, more and more are needed and will be constructed. But by the way, how are things going in your country?"

✓ **For rebuking questions or aggressive questions**, the speaker should reply firmly and politely. For example, to the question "Since many companies including IBM and Microsoft are developing new versions of Data Conference tools, don't you think what you do is completely useless?", you could answer, "I've noticed your saying … I'm sorry to bring this up, but you seem to have had a misunderstanding of our work. I think, each person has his or her own merits as well as weak points. As to weak points, one shouldn't have analyzed things one-sidedly and only by analogy. So, with what you said, I'm afraid, you might have made a mistake in logic …"

As shown above, euphemism like "so far", "possible", "I think", "personal" and "reference" is often used in questions and answers. The usage of euphemism can meet two purposes. Firstly, the speaker's answer to the raised questions is not 100% affirmative, which accords with the nature of science that science can only tell the truth in a certain context. Since the scientific research results are affected by many factors, the results will change with any one of the factors. Additionally, speakers are modest and use euphemism to close the distance between them and the audience.

The following are tips to answering questions at international academic conferences:
- Listen to the questions clearly (so as to ensure they are exchanging on the same question)
- Judge questions correctly (so as to know the real purpose of the question and make answers accordingly)

- Copy the original question pattern
- Repeat the related content from the previous presentation
- Ask back the question
- Answer questions partially (when time is limited)
- Leave room for improvement

Sample 1	
MR. PRINCE: **We do have time for a couple of questions before wrap-up, so let's go right here** (pointing to someone in the audience) first.	Opening
QUESTIONER 1: **A couple of questions. One is for** Dr. Myers, **the other one for** Dr. Flaherty.	Raising a question
Dr. Myers, **it's quite impressive to** observe the number of the drop in incidence of errors, but **do you have any indication** yet as **to** what that 6.7 percent may be pointing at?	
DR. MYERS: **I'm not sure that I understand your question.**	Asking to repeat the question
QUESTIONER 1: Well, there's still an incidence of 6.7 percent, although down from 28 percent. As you look at the 6.7 percent, is there any indication yet as to what the causes of those are?	
DR. MYERS: No. I only have anecdotal data which is not scientifically based. But there has been a reduction, a further reduction in medication errors. **I guess that's what you're asking me, right**?	Confirming the question
QUESTIONER I: Exactly. But, you know, **I'm interested in** the causes of the remaining 6.7.	
DR. MYERS: Oh. Oh, okay.	
QUESTIONER 1: You know, is it human factors? Is it technical? Are they—?	
DR. MYERS: **I don't have that information.**	Admitting he (she) cannot answer the question
QUESTIONER 1: Okay. All right. All right.	
And, Dr. Flaherty, you know, you mentioned a number of issues where research has been done, human factors being one of them, and others. Are you aware, or do you have any source you can share with me, of somebody who might be doing research in the area of knowledge? How much does knowledge have to do—how much is the impact of knowledge on the consequences, of outcomes in the practice of medicine? Is anybody looking at that you know of?	Commenting

DR. FLAHERTY: **There is some insight.** I think the problem is that because of this culture of medical perfection that we live in, that when we see someone that has failed in some way, or whoever the finger is pointed at as the identified cause, is not usually knowledge-based. It's usually system-based. That's a setup for trouble. So I don't think anybody has made that identification. **Certainly, there is an issue of scope, but I don't think that's really the issue here.** I think it's mostly system's errors. QUESTIONER 1: Thank you. MR. PRINCE: Dick Wannamaker?	Answering the question
QUESTIONER 2: **I have one question, and it is for** Dr. Bagian. I have read your article about safety, and I was impressed by some of the issues that you did not bring up at this point. One of them is that you talked about data collection, and some of them are real and some of them may be distorted. And the other is that once the data is collected, it should be non-punitive and should be considered, and I would like to ask you to expand on these issues.	Asking a question
DR. BAGIAN: **Well, if I understood your question correctly, you want to know** how we do our data collection, and what we —. QUESTIONER 2: I think you mentioned in your article, I believe, that some of what was reported as adverse reaction was not a safety issue. DR. BAGIAN: Oh, okay. QUESTIONER 2: We didn't have an input in it, and it was counted as —.	Confirming the question
DR. BAGIAN: Okay. **I think what you're referring to is the fact that** probably out of the *New York Times* article, where I said 2,974 errors occurred and 714 deaths.	Confirming again
QUESTIONER 2: Right. DR. BAGIAN: And it said they were due to errors, and that's not true. What we had was, in our system we'd like to know anything that people think might be an error, an adverse event; it doesn't have to be an error—we still want to know about it.	Answering it
MR. PRINCE: **Any additional questions from the floor?** **If so, please ask.** **Hearing no questions and not seeing anyone at a mike, I'd like to thank the panel and give them a round of applause.**	Ending

Sample 2	
MR. CIMMNO: **I'd like to open it up now and have a question and answer session and a round-table discussion if we could**. If you could, please speak into the microphones. We're all being recorded here. Yes.	Opening
Questioner 1: **My name is** Russ Hayward. **I'm with Mobile Oil Corporation, and I wanted to thank all of you for your presentations**. They were excellent, but the question I have for you, Chico, is relative to these task teams. Are they from each department or a craft group?	Self-introduction; Asking a question
MR. McGill: We have different types of task teams. Some of them are from the same department. For instance, we might have a welding task team, or a fitting task team, all from the same trade. Then we have other task teams for a particular vessel or a particular building where we might have a sheet metal building task team or we might have a sea lift task team. So different types, some of them are in the same trade, some of them cross-functional.	Answering the question
Questioner 1: Okay. Thank you.	
MR. CIMMINO: Thanks, Chico. **Another question**?	Inviting for more questions;
Questioner 2: Yeah, **I'm** Sean Gallagher **from NIOSH**, and most of what you were talking about is dealing with the process of building the ship itself. **I was wondering**, do you deal with people who design the ships in order to make some of these types of changes come about?	Self-introduction; Asking a question
MR. CIMMNO: **Are we talking about** the people actually using the ship?	Confirming the question
Questioner 2: Yeah, yeah. The people using the ship or the people designing the ship to make some of these processes work.	
MR. CMMMNO: I haven't done that. I concentrate on the workers building the ship, and we haven't gotten involved in the usage of the ship with the exception—as I said earlier, when you work on a ship, you're essentially repeating processes in its manufacture. So when you make it easier to build, you then make it easier to maintain. So that aspect, yes. But the using of the ship aspect, no. **Either of you have a comment on that**?	Answering the question Inviting other speakers to answer
MR. Ziegfried: Well, one of the things that the Panel talked about was the fact that you have to look at the idea of the end product and what you're using in designing safety into those aspects of things. You know, we're hoping that that's something that they look at in the study they do, that we're trying to get together. You know, whether that comes about or not, I'm not really sure. But certainly the question has been asked by that panel, and we are looking at that aspect.	Answering it

Questioner 2: Thank you. MR. CIMMINO: **Any other questions**? One more. Questioner 3: Joy Flack **with** OSHA. **I want to make one comment.** There's a lot of talk about employee involvement, but employee involvement without employee empowerment, you soon lose the involvement. So I think you probably need to use both of those terms. And then the other question I have is when you had the VPP (Voluntary Protection Program) reviews at your facility, did they address ergonomics at their VPP or is that anything that you did on your own? MR. CMMNO: Okay. **I'll hit those one at a time. You're 100 percent correct in that** without employee empowerment, involvement is useless. And if you really want to knock the wind out of a group of people, ask them to study a problem and then ignore their results. So absolutely, employee empowerment is critical. And as far as the VPP, yes, they did look at the ergonomic program, and they awarded us a star. So they must have been happy with it. Any other questions?	**Inviting for the last question** **Self-introduction;** **Asking a question**
MR CMMINO: Well, **thank you very much. I hope this was as good a session for you as it was for us.** If you have any questions, we will be up here for a few minutes right now before lunch.	**Ending**

Exercises

❶ **Read Samples 1 & 2 and answer the following questions.**

(1) What is the basic pattern of Q & A session?

(2) What might be the motivations of asking questions?

(3) What will the speaker do to answer the questions?

(4) What might be an appropriate way if the speaker knows little about the question raised?

❷ **Refer to the expressions in the textbook and translate the following into English.**

(1) 在结束之前我们有几分钟的提问时间。

_____

_____

(2) 我是北京大学的张宇。首先谢谢各位演讲人的讲话,非常精彩。但是我有一个问题想请教顾教授。

___

(3) 对不起,我没听清你的问题。能不能请你重复一遍?

___

(4) 如果我理解得没错,你是想问我们是怎样进行数据收集的。

___

(5) 对不起,对于你问的这个问题我恐怕了解得太少,因为我们的重点不是放在这方面。

___

(6) 你的这一个问题大概包含了五点内容。我想就你说的最后一点谈一下。如果我概括得不对,请告诉我。

___

(7) 谢谢你的问题,希望你对我的回答感到满意。

___

(8) 还有其他的问题吗?好吧,谢谢各位的耐心,也谢谢大家愿意和我们分享经验。希望各位下午过得愉快。

___

❸ Complete the transcript of the Q & A period in the conference titled "Ergonomics: Effective Workplace Practices and Programs".

(Dr. Bran Peacock is the moderator as well as a speaker, and Dr. Bill Marras is a speaker.)

Dr. Peacock: (1) _____
_____
(现在各位如果有任何问题的话,可以提出来,我想我们只有几分钟的提问时间。谁先开始? 好的,我们有了一个提问人。请说。).

Questioner 1: (2) _____
(我有一个问题想请教 Bill Marras 博士). (3) _____ (我很喜欢你的发言) and the multimedia associated with it. (4) _____ (我的问题是) the problems that I've seen in the warehouse industry have a lot to do with timing issues and time standards. And (5) _____ (我想知道你是不是) had addressed that portion of the research.

Dr. Marras: We have considered that a constant in this. I know what you're talking about. A lot of times these people are really pushed by performance standards. We observed that warehouses work people at 125 boxes per hour. We did not look at this as a variable in this initial study.

Questioner 1: Well, I see. Thank you.

Questioner 2: Question for you, Brian. (6) _____ (我叫 Ed Fredericks, 是 Michigan OSHA 的 industrial hygienist). The corporate-wide settlement between GM, UAW and OSHA is winding down, and I know from our experience, we see plants that have done very well and then plants that have not done so well. Are you a part of or are you aware of any type of report card kind of thing that GM, UAW or OSHA will be producing as the agreement wears down?

Dr. Peacock: (7) _____ (对不起,我不能回答这个问题). I am not part of that joint activity. I exist in the engineering function which deals mainly with proactive design, and you're referring to a joint UAW-GM-OSHA reactive program. At the moment, the discussion of its continuance or the report card is up in the air. So I'm afraid I can't answer that question.

Questioner 2: Okay. Thank you anyway.

Questioner 3: I'm Monica Steele from Abbott Laboratories, and (8) _____ (这个问题谁来回答都可以) I'm wondering if there is one tool that you would give a mechanical design engineer, be it one of the NIOSH models or a bio-mechanical model. Which it might be that you would have the most confidence in? Not only the results, but given the fact that these engineers may not be trained in ergonomics and may not use it properly. (9) _____ (换句话说), which tool is most likely for them not to make a drastic error and to come out with some reasonable results? Or do you think I ought to stand firm on some numbers that I have from my analysis?

Dr. Marras: Well, (10) _____ (我想,你的问题是) how important it is to be 100 percent right? What I would recommend is to base it on the very simple concept of moments. If it's too far away, you can't handle so much weight. If it's too high, you can't handle too much weight. If it's low enough, you can handle so much weight. And that's probably the simplest and easiest thing to do. Keep it simple.

> **Questioner 3**: Keep it simple. Okay. Thank you.
>
> **DR. Peacock**: (11) _____ (这个问题的一种回答是) that we're forever asking questions of that nature, and the approach that we use is a consensus of experts to come up with the number. (12) _____
> _____
>
> (好吧,谢谢大家花时间来关注这次会议。我非常感谢。我很遗憾地宣布提问只能到此结束。谢谢你们提出这么富有启发性的问题,我很乐意在会后和大家继续探讨。)

Useful Expressions and Sentence Patterns

1. For Questioners

(1) Self-Introduction

> My name is ***. I'm an (*ergonomic consultant*) with (*the Saunders Group, Minneapolis*).
> I am *** I work with (*OSHA*).
> I'm … from (*the University of Hawaii*).
> I am … of (*USA Today*).

(2) Raising Questions

> I would like to raise a question to Mr. ***.
> Dr. ***, may/could/might I ask you three questions?
> My question concerns / is concerned with / has to do with …
> My second question is the following.
> There are several questions I would like to ask Mr. ***.
> Mr. ***, I wonder if you would be good/kind enough to explain …
> I'd be grateful for any comments you may care to make about ABC.
> A couple of questions. One is for Dr. ***, the other one for Dr. ***.
> (*Dr. ****), you know, you mentioned a number of issues (*where research has been done, human factors being one of them, and others*). (*Are you aware, or*) do you have any source you can share with me, of (*somebody who might be doing research in the area of knowledge*)?
> (*I wanted to thank all of you for your presentations. They were excellent, but*) the question I have for you, (*Dr. ***,*) is relative to (*these task teams*).
> And then the other question I have is (*when you had the VPP reviews at your facility, did they address ergonomics at their VPP or is that something that you did on your own?*)

➢ I'm wondering if any of you could address whether (*these issues come up explicitly in your ergonomics committees*), or if they just kind of happen without anybody thinking about (*them*).

➢ I have two questions and they're for Dr. ***. The first question is (*the problems that I've seen in the warehouse industry have a lot to do with timing issues and time standards*). And I was wondering whether or not (*you had addressed that portion of the research*).

➢ My question is for anyone on the panel who'd like to jump on it.

➢ (I don't know if I need the microphone, but Pat Hirschberg is being very quiet.) Would you like to tell us your story about (*the chairs as far as the motivator*)?

➢ I have one more question, and I am not sure who would be the best to answer it. But how do you (*retrofit these really old sewing machines that— you know, the old black metal kind*)?

➢ I was just going to say that, Dr. ***, in your presentation you talked about (*how you went from another health and safety pattern into ergonomics*). I was going to ask the other panelists if (*using the worker involvement model in ergonomics has helped other health and safety problems in your plants using that model*).

➢ I have a question for Dr. ***. You mentioned (*—you showed a sewing machine with some arm supports*). I didn't really understand that. Could you explain that a little bit more?

➢ Dr. ***, I have a question for you. I would like to know what (*tricks or motivation you had when you were able to convince management that they really needed to deal with their program*).

➢ I have a specific question, Dr. ***, and I don't know if it is a problem with time or what. But I was wondering whether (*there were any different equipment engineering controls you use, aside from the stretching and the back belts and that type of thing*).

➢ One more question. You referred to (*periodic retraining*). Was that (*periodic retraining with your stretching program and the back prevention program*)? And to what extent was that?

➢ I guess my next question (*then, differently, to go off to something else*) is: (*Are people being compensated for their extra work load?*)

➢ I wanted to ask a question. I thought it was very interesting in your presentation, Dr. ***, about (*the equal participation of union members* and the management members of the team). I was just wondering if the other panelists could comment on (*their numbers*).

➢ I have to admit that your presentations have been one of the most entertaining that I have seen through the whole day, so kudos to you all. This is a question directed to Dr. ∗∗∗ and relates to (*the patient transfer teams*). Could you give us a little more insight into (*the dynamics of the team*)?

➢ A question to Dr. ∗∗∗ regarding the surveys you do, (*are they anonymous surveys?*)

➢ I would like to hear what (*CWA*) has to say about that.

(3) **Clarifying Questions**

➢ Do you see what I'm getting at?

➢ That's not what I was really asking. What I was getting at was …

➢ Let me put this another way.

➢ Let me put to you another situation—suppose …

➢ I'd just like to repeat that.

➢ Perhaps I didn't really make my question clear. In fact, what I asked was …

➢ I understand that, but what I really want to know is …

➢ Yes, that's true but what about …

➢ Well, perhaps you've got a point there, but …

➢ Have I made that clear?

2. For Presenters

(1) **Confirming Questions**

➢ I'm not sure that I understand your question.

➢ I'm sorry. I didn't hear you clearly. What's your last point, please?

➢ I beg your pardon?

➢ I would like to have the second question repeated, for I didn't really understand it.

➢ Sorry, but I'm not sure what your question is.

➢ I guess that's what you're asking me, right?

➢ Well, I guess the question is how important it is to be 100% right.

➢ Well, if I understood your question correctly, you want to know (*how we do our data collection*).

➢ Are we talking about (*the people actually using the ship*)?

➢ So you are asking (*beyond the question of Jerusalem*) or (*in the context*)?

➢ Sorry. I didn't quite get your question. Could you clarify your first point,

please?
- I don't quite follow what you were saying. Would you please repeat your question?
- I'm afraid I didn't understand that. Could you repeat what you just said?
- I didn't catch that. Could you repeat that, please?
- I missed that. Could you say it again, please?
- Could you run that by me one more time?
- I don't quite follow you. What exactly do you mean?
- I'm afraid I don't quite understand what you are getting at.
- Could you explain to me how (*that is going to work*)?
- I don't see what you mean. Could we have some more details, please?

(2) **Answering the Questions**
- That's an excellent observation, and I completely endorse your observation.
- That is a good question, (*and I think the lady, the one in front of you, also had a point to that, too*).
- You asked a lot of questions there, and they were all excellent.
- I think you hit the nail on the head.
- That's an interesting/important question.
- I think that is a key/difficult/complicated/hard question.
- I appreciate that question.
- Thank you for (asking) that question.
- If I understand your question correctly, I can say that …
- I think Dr. ✳✳✳'s question is really to the point.
- Yes. I'd be delighted to.
- Certainly/Surely.
- I would like to answer Mr. ✳✳✳'s question.
- Let me first reply to the first question.
- May I answer your second question first?
- My answer to that question is that …
- Let me try to answer these questions one by one.
- No. I don't think I would say that (*I think it is a combination of that plus individual task training*).
- I think that is a key question and I think the answer is no, (*they are not widely appreciated*). I don't know if other people have other suggestions on what we can do.
- It is a difficult question because I presume (*you are in a state where the*

employee has the right to select a physician). Is that correct?
- I hope I am making sense to you, but it is a tough question.
- If I may, I know the question wasn't addressed to me, but I would echo the same thing.
- You have about five things in (*one question*). I'd like to come to the last one that you talked about. (*If I encapsulate it incorrectly, tell me.*)
- Okay. I'll hit those one at a time. You are 100 percent correct in that (*without employee empowerment, involvement is useless*).
- I will address this question and discuss the first question that was asked of Dr. *** about (*frequency*).
- One answer to that question is (*that we're forever asking questions of that nature, and the approach that we use is a consensus of experts to come up with the number*).
- Well, let me try to answer that (*from a general perspective*).
- To answer your questions—I didn't understand your question initially. You were asking if (*we believed that physical ability testing is effective*). The answer is (*absolutely yes*).
- I think we have a multi-part question here. First, to address the (*facilities*) issues (*and charges back to facilities, in many cases that may be inappropriate because facilities only set the stage*).
- The second part of your question is (*statistics*) ... And as soon as they give it to me, I would be happy to share some statistics with you, if you would leave me your business card.

(3) **Knowing Little About the Issue Raised**
- I'm afraid I know little about the question you asked. To justify this, we need more information for further explanation. Sorry.
- Let's get some other questions. We will definitely get your question answered.
- I can't say a lot about it. I have not studied it. (*I have heard pros and cons with it.*)
- No, I cannot address that question.
- I'm afraid I can't answer that question.
- It is a difficult question. I'm afraid my answer cannot give you a satisfactory explanation.
- Sorry, I don't have that information.
- There is an issue of (*scope*), but I don't think that's really the issue here.

- Sorry. I have had little experience with this problem, since our emphasis is not laid on this point.
- Would you mind if I dealt with that question later?
- That's not anything I've had time to deal with.
- Would anybody else like to comment on this?
- That's a very interesting question, but it's not anything I've looked into.
- You're quite right. I hadn't thought about that aspect.
- I'm afraid what you asked is beyond the point. It seems that it is not pertinent to our present topic.
- While it is an important issue, it's too complex to deal with here.

(4) **Showing Agreement**
- I would agree with that.
- I agree.
- I couldn't agree more.
- You've got a point here.
- Absolutely. / Definitely. / Precisely. / Exactly.
- That's how I see it, too.
- That's my opinion, too.
- I think so, too. Me, too.
- Of course.
- That's true / right / for sure.
- Exactly.
- I totally agree with you.
- That's exactly the way I feel.
- Thank you. I concur with you.

(5) **Showing Disagreement**
- I don't agree.
- I can't quite agree with you.
- I don't think so at all.
- I'm afraid not.
- I don't think you are right.
- It can't be true.
- I'm inclined to disagree with you on that.
- I have to disagree.
- I'm sorry, I can't agree with you in saying that.
- I think I am quite in disagreement with you.

- That's not what I'm saying.
- Unfortunately, I see it differently.
- Up to a point I agree with you, but in practice, things just do not work that way.
- I'm afraid I can't agree.

(6) Asking Whether the Answer Is Satisfactory

- This is my answer. Is it enough for your question?
- This is my opinion. What do you think of it?
- Thank you for your questions. I hope you are satisfied with my answers.
- Are you satisfied with my answer?
- I don't know if this is a satisfactory answer.
- Did that answer your question?
- I think that might be the answer to your question.
- I hope I am making sense to you, but it is a tough question.

3. For Chairpersons

(1) Declaring It Is Time for Raising Questions

- We have several minutes for questions. If you could, please go to the mike and ask a specific question of one or more of the panelists.
- Okay, I appreciate your attending the session and listening and giving your attention to the speakers. We shared some ideas and thoughts with you. We have tried to share some things that have worked well within the organizations that we worked with. Now, it is time for a dialogue. I would be happy to hear ideas and concepts that you have, as well as questions that you may have. If you would, please step to the microphone and identify yourself and your organization for the record.
- Any questions or comments? If you can, come to the floor microphone, please.
- Now, I think we have just a few minutes for any questions that anyone might have. Who would like to lead off? Okay, we have one. Go ahead.
- I know it's very close to (three o'clock), but we're willing to stay until the break time if you guys are willing to do that and especially if you have any questions or comments for any of our three panelists.
- Well, we have such a crowded program, we don't have a lot of time for questions, but we do have some time and I hope we will have some discussion if we can get people from the audience who may want to contribute some of their experiences in (the construction industry of things that they have noticed that could be done to reduce the risk of ergonomics

injuries). Does anybody want to get up? Any questions?
- (*Can we get the lights, please?*) I guess we will open the floor now to questions and answers.
- Well, that is probably a record. (*One ex-university professor and two university professors*) finished (*15*) minutes ahead of time. There will be (*15*) minutes for questions for anybody who has questions. I think this afternoon. We have said some very different things and some contradictory things. And so, one would hope that there might be some questions.
- We have a few minutes for questions. I would like to invite any questions for Dr. *** first, because he is going to have to leave to catch a plane. (*Is your question for Dr. ***?*) (*Would you go to the microphone, please?*)
- This is an opportunity for any questions, comments, or concerns you may have of the speakers. (*From the audience? Yes, in the back?*)
- Okay. Any questions? We have about (*ten*) minutes. I would like to kind of go over here now, and we will pull together any questions and answers.
- Let's go ahead and open things up to the audience here. (*That gentleman, do you have a question? Could you direct it to whoever?*)

(2) **Inviting Questions from Audience**
- Let me call on the next question, if I may, so we are moving questions around. (*To the microphone at the back of the room, please?*)
- Any other questions?
- Any other questions or comments?
- Any additional questions?
- Next question?
- We have time for one more question, and you are it.
- Any additional questions? Let's take this as the last question.
- One last question. / Let's have one last question.
- Our allocated time is almost up. Now I would like to answer one more question.
- Any other questions? One more.
- Dr. ***, last quick question.
- One or two more questions. I think you were next.
- Any additional questions? Let's take this as the last question.

(3) **Inviting the Presenter to Answer**
- Either of you want to comment on that?
- Dr. ***, did you have a comment?

- Do any of you want to comment on that?
- Dr. ***, would you like to comment?
- Any other quick comments on (*those two questions*), or should we proceed to the next one?
- Let's get comments from any of you on (*those*). Dr. ***, do you want to start?
- Any other comment on that? Dr. ***, you might want to comment on (*the American side*) on (*the political question*).
- Anybody?
- Any other final comments?
- Does anyone else want to respond to (*Susan's first part about the ad*)?

(4) **Ending the Conference**

- Any additional questions from the floor? If so, please ask. Hearing no question and not seeing anybody at a mike, I'd like to thank the panel and suggest we give them a round of appreciation.
- Okay, well, thank you all for your attention and your time. I appreciate it very much. I am sorry to say that this session will have to stop here. Thank you for your illuminating questions. I would be very glad to discuss them with you after the meeting.
- With that, I would like to close the session by thanking the speakers, (*Dr. *** of Lowes Company, Dr. *** of J. C. Penney, and Dr. ***, Jr. of Murphy Warehouse*).
- Thanks a lot. Why don't we conclude this session? Thanks for your patience in allowing us to run a few minutes over. Certainly, if you have any questions, the presenters are still here and there are also papers that were left on the registration table. Thank you.
- I think I've got to draw this session to a close. But before I draw it to a close, I've got to thank (*Dr. *** from NIOSH*) for putting this session together and getting us all to come to talk. (*Again, thank you very much, Dr. ****.*) And thank you all for coming.
- Any other questions? Well, we do appreciate your patience and willingness to share with us your experiences as well. I hope that you enjoy the rest of the afternoon. Drive safely or fly safely.
- Thanks very much for coming and have a good lunch.
- Well, thank you very much. I hope this was as good a session for you as it was for us. If you have any questions, we will be up here for a few minutes right

now before lunch.
- ➤ Additional questions from anyone in the audience? If not, on behalf of (*the three of us*), we greatly appreciated all of your interaction with us.

Manners and Etiquette

Warm-up

1. What preparations should we make for conference participation?
2. What manners are appropriate for conference attendees? And what are inappropriate? Please list some examples.

Academic conferences are formal activities and demand appropriate etiquette and manners from the participants. Normally, the following 6 guidelines should be obeyed: (1) arrive early and be prepared; (2) dress properly; (3) be respectful and thoughtful; (4) don't be too quick to react; (5) own his stage and watch his body language; (6) be prepared for the unexpected.

1. Arrive Early and Be Prepared

The speaker should arrive about an hour before he delivers his presentation.

Showing up early can ensure his preparedness. Besides, the time needs to be considered to park, to find the presentation location, to deal with equipment set-up and testing, etc.

2. Dress Properly

The way the speaker dresses will reflect not only himself, but everything he is representing. Dress for the event, but don't overdo it. Take into consideration the audience and the purpose of the presentation to best select the dress code. For instance, a dark-colored dress or suit with tie will do. Never wear anything too fancy.

3. Be Respectful and Thoughtful

Being an expert or an academic presenter does not give room for being conceited. Honorific words like "please", "thank you" are often used. Respect the audience and wait for others to complete a thought. The speaker also needs to bear in mind that the audience's time is valuable. Never talk too much. Respect their time and make sure that in exchange for the time they devote, that constant value is provided throughout the presentation. Make the words clear, follow tightly the key words and make the speech efficient.

4. Don't Be Too Quick to React

Fast reaction seems like the speaker is on the defensive side. Allow a brief second for questions or reactions from the audience to set in. There is magic in a pause. A brief 3-second pause is never noticed by the audience and it gives the speaker time to breathe, think, and react. Reacting too fast can cause fillers, like "ums" and "ahs", or make the speaker seem rash.

5. Own the Stage and Watch the Body Language

Own the stage. This goes back to arriving early and having time to know the space he has to work with. He'd better move around it so he can address every part of the room.

The body language he uses on the stage also aids in conveying his message. Keep it precise and simple. Every movement should have a specific purpose. Don't just move for the sake of moving.

6. Be Prepared for the Unexpected

Unless he has psychic abilities and can see into the future, the speaker doesn't know when the unexpected is coming.

Be prepared for the worst case scenarios. The speaker should know the material in case there is a problem where he can't use the visual aid. Or, even the backup files should have backup files.

Relax and present to the individuals. Maybe the initial schedule is to present to a small group and now it is an entire auditorium.

The above relates to the general etiquette principles for the conference speakers and lecturers. For other conference participants, conferences are also wonderful learning experiences, during which the education and connections will happen naturally. In the process of connection, a few tips can help avoid any embarrassing, or even costly, mistakes. They are:

- **At the Opening Reception**

Prior to attending the conference, the participant should do homework and figure out who he would like to meet and see over the next few days. Scan through the welcome packet and highlight any names of people he'd like to see. Upon arrival, make it a mission to network with the highlighted attendees.

The participant should not come so hungry to attack the bar and food area as soon as he arrives. Networking is the time to meet and greet, and then eat and drink. About a half hour before the opening reception, get a snack. Make it something light but filling, like an apple or a smoothie. The purpose of this event is to meet and greet people, which can be difficult when carrying a drink and a plate.

When alone at the networking or opening session, the participant may start off by approaching another individual or small group of two to three people. It can be awkward to approach a larger group, as they are harder to break into and to start a one-on-one conversation. After the initial conversations, ask the new contacts to have a drink or meet near the buffet for food.

The participant could move around the room. When he meets someone, introduce himself, exchange business cards, talk, possibly set-up another time to meet or a time for a call after return. Shake hands as he leaves, thank them and then move on to the next person.

- **At General Sessions or Parallel Sessions**

Notebook paper and pens should be prepared ahead. If the participant forgot to bring some, he could find a notepad in the hotel room or at the front desk, but it's better to be prepared ahead of time.

Don't take up two or three seats. The participant may move right on in and meet someone new, sitting next to him. Make a self-introduction briefly. Enjoy their company before the speaker begins. Arrive early, sit in the front and learn as much as he can.

This is a time to learn. If the participant is with a chatty attendee, he may politely tell them that he would love to talk after the session. Be polite, sincere and firm. Tell them right at the beginning of the conversation. If he waits too long to say something, he can get hooked into the conversation, and it will be more uncomfortable to get out.

Respect the speaker. For a speaker, it can be frustrating to be on a stage in front of a group and realize attendees are chatting amongst themselves. If the participant must have a conversation or make a phone call, he can leave the room out of respect.

- **In Networking Events**

Bring some name cards. The purpose should be to meet and hopefully bring back opportunities for further cooperation.

Start and end each conversation with a handshake. Always stand up when meeting someone to shake hands.

Making small talk is easy, even if the participant is shy by nature. Ask people about when they arrived, their travel, their hometown, and the weather; talk about the conference or the speakers. These topics open up the conversation; just avoid any emotional topics such as politics or religion.

Projects

Project 1: *Oral Presentation, Group Work with 5 Members*

Work cooperatively to prepare a conference presentation speech on "Innovation of Technology" in the **International Conference on Innovation of Technology**. The speech can be based on your own research, or on others' research papers. However, the research is conducted, and you should make efforts to learn every detail of the research and then present to the whole class.

The presentation speech consists of 5 parts:

Part One: Introduction and Background (about 3 minutes)

Part Two: Literature Review (about 2 minutes)

Part Three: Methodology (about 3 minutes)

Part Four: Findings and Discussion (about 7 minutes)

Part Five: Summary/Conclusions/Implications/Predictions (about 3 minutes)

Q & A (Questions and Answers) takes about 2 minutes.

Project 2: *Oral Presentation, Independent Work*

Students in one class are usually from different disciplines or majors. Please make an oral presentation of 3 – 5 minutes to introduce your research to the class. A PPT is preferred with gist only. Bear in mind that the classmates might have very limited knowledge of your research area and try to use less professional terms and more examples to make you understood by the classmates. Three-Minute Thesis

(3MT) and Five-Minute Research Presentation (5MRP) could be good references for you.

3MT

The **Three-Minute Thesis** (3MT) is an academic competition that assists current graduate students in fostering effective presentation and communication skills. Participants have only three minutes to explain the breadth and significance of their research project to a non-specialist audience. 3MT was developed by the University of Queensland in 2008, and is now held at many countries around the world.

5MRP

Five-Minute Research Presentation (5MRP) is a national competition held by China Academic English Teaching Association. The purpose is to improve the ability of Chinese undergraduate and graduate students to conduct research innovation and academic communication in English, and to help future Chinese researchers effectively introduce their research ideas to their international counterparts. The competition has been hailed as an important innovation in China's shift from General English (EGP) to Academic English (EAP) in college English teaching.

Presentation Assessment Form

	Profile A	Profile B	Profile C	Profile D
Delivery	1. Pronunciation hardly interferes with comprehension. 2. Volume and speed are appropriate. 3. Rhythm and intonation are varied and appropriate. 4. Good eye contact.	1. Pronunciation of individual words occasionally interferes with comprehension. 2. Volume and speed are adequate. 3. Rhythm and intonation are generally appropriate. 4. Eye contact may be limited.	1. Pronunciation of chunks of language at times makes comprehension impossible. 2. Volume/speed may be inadequate, and there is little or no eye contact. 3. May be inappropriate use of gesture.	1. Pronunciation and intonation frequently impede comprehension, making it difficult to evaluate the presentation. 2. May be inaudible.
Language	1. Clear evidence of ability to express complex ideas, using a wide range of appropriate vocabulary. 2. Cohesive devices, where used, contribute to fluency. 3. High degree of grammatical accuracy.	1. Some ability to express complex ideas, although not consistently. 2. Reasonable use of range of vocabulary and structures. 3. Cohesive devices, where used, contribute to fluency, but are sometimes misapplied.	1. Rang of vocabulary and structures are adequate to express simple ideas. 2. Errors sometimes impede communication.	1. Very limited range of vocabulary and grammar means that ideas are expressed with difficulty. 2. Presentation is often repetitive, due to insufficient control of language.

continued

	Profile A	Profile B	Profile C	Profile D
Organization	1. Strong introduction, with clear outline. 2. Logical ordering of main points. 3. Effective conclusion.	1. Generally, there is a logical ordering of main ideas. 2. Introduction/conclusion are linked with main points.	1. Presentation lacks clear organization of ideas, making it difficult to follow.	1. Lack of any apparent organization makes it difficult to follow presentation.
Content	1. Content is appropriate and relevant. 2. Topic is explored in sufficient depth.	1. Content is mostly appropriate and relevant.	1. Content is at times irrelevant, and development of ideas is superficial.	1. Content is not always related to the topic and there is little development of ideas.
Evidence of Preparation	1. Evidence often with thorough familiarity with topic. 2. Fluent delivery, with skillful use of notes. Dealing well with questions. 3. Using PowerPoint enhances the presentation.	1. Familiar with topic. 2. Use of notes sometimes interferes with delivery of presentation. 3. Use of PowerPoint at times distracts from presentation content, due to unclear script / inappropriate pictures / poor timing.	1. Reasonable presentation. 2. Organization mostly clear and logical. 3. Acceptable use of visual aids. 4. Some difficulty in dealing with questions.	1. Inadequate preparation, with little evidence of familiarity with subject. 2. Visual aids unhelpful, unclear or ineffective. 3. Too much focus on PowerPoint rather than basic content. 4. Inability to deal with questions.

References

[1] Bruce, I. Syllabus design for general EAP writing courses: A cognitive approach [J]. *Journal of English for Academic Purposes*, 2005, 4 (3): 239 –256.

[2] Hyland, K. *Disciplinary Discourses: Social Interactions in Academic Writing* [M]. Michigan: University of Michigan Press, 2004.

[3] Hyland, K. Specificity revisited: How far should we go now? [J]. *English for Specific Purposes*, 2002, 21: 385 –395.

[4] Jordan, R. R. *English for Academic Purposes* (EAP) [M]. Cambridge: Cambridge University Press, 1997.

[5] Nunan, D. *Task-based Language Teaching* [M]. Cambridge: Cambridge University Press, 2004.

[6] Stoller, F. L. Project work: A means to promote language and content [A]. In J. C. Richards & W. A. Renandya (eds.). *Methodolody in Language Teaching: An Anthology of Current Practice* [C]. Cambridge: Cambridge University Press. 2002: 107 –120.

[7] 常乐,吴明海,徐培文. 基于学术英语理念的建筑工程类国际学术交流英语课程设置研究[J]. 中国ESP研究, 2017, 8(2): 110 –118,164.

[8] 陈美华. 学术交流英语[M]. 北京:外语教学与研究出版社, 2013.

[9] 从丛,王文宇. 学术交流英语教程(第2版)[M]. 南京:南京大学出版社, 2014.

[10] 范娜. 国际学术交流英语[M]. 北京:清华大学出版社, 2019.

[11] 郭继荣. 国际学术交流英语[M]. 西安:西安交通大学出版社, 2012.

[12] 韩媛媛. 国际学术交流英语教学中跨文化交际能力的培养[J]. 大学教育, 2020 (6): 20 –23,27.

[13] 洪卫. 学术交际英语[M]. 北京:电子工业出版社, 2012.

[14] 胡庚申. 国际会议交流[M]. 北京:外语教学与研究出版社, 2013.

[15] 贾卫国. 国际学术交流英语[M]. 北京:外语教学与研究出版社, 2008.

[16] 姜怡,姜欣. 学术交流英语[M]. 北京:高等教育出版社, 2006.

[17] 李琼花. 通用学术交流英语[M]. 厦门:厦门大学出版社, 2019.

[18] 李文梅. 研究生学术交流英语[M]. 北京:清华大学出版社,2021.

[19] 欧洲理事会文化合作教育委员会. 欧洲语言共同参考框架:学习、教学、评估[M]. 刘骏,傅荣,主译. 北京:外语教学与研究出版社,2008.

[20] 王春岩. 全球20所大学学术英语能力内涵调查及对我国的启示[J]. 解放军外国语学院学报,2019,42(3):56-63.

[21] 王春岩,杨翠萍. 学术写作中体裁意识的培养与语体特征的转变[J]. 中国外语教育,2017(1):31-37.

[22] 王慧莉,贾卫国. 国际学术交流英语[M]. 大连:大连理工大学出版社,2005.

[23] 王哲. 英语学术讲座与交流[M]. 广州:中山大学出版社,2018.

[24] 卫乃兴. 学术英语再思考:理论、路径与方法[J]. 现代外语,2016(2):267-277.

[25] 吴斐,周频. 国际学术交流英语[M]. 武汉:武汉大学出版社,2008.

[26] 夏纪梅. 论高校大学学术英语课程的建构[J]. 外语教学理论与实践,2014(1):6-9.

[27] 杨安良,周大军. 研究生学术交流英语能力体系构建研究[J]. 当代教育理论与实践,2018,10(2):131-136.

[28] 张锦涛. 国际学术交流实用英语教程[M]. 北京:国防工业出版社,2006.

[29] 张俊梅. 基于项目驱动的非英语专业博士研究生英语教学模式研究——以国际会议交流英语课程为例[J]. 学位与研究生教育,2014(10):31-35.

[30] 张荔. 学术英语交流——写作与演讲[M]. 上海:上海交通大学出版社,2017.

[31] 张萍. 小组协作—项目驱动—任务分解——硕士研究生学术英语交流能力培养的教改实践[J]. 学位与研究生教育,2013(7):33-37.

[32] 赵鸿雁. 学术交流英语口语[M]. 上海:上海交通大学出版社,2014.

[33] 周大军,杨安良. 研究生学术交流英语能力培养的优化途径——整体任务型教学模式探索[J]. 高等教育研究学报,2018,41(1):38-43.

[34] 周红红,绳丽惠,郭海云. 基于建构主义理论的博士生学术交流英语课程设计[J]. 学位与研究生教育,2011(2):40-44.

[35] 周梅. 项目驱动下理工科博士生英语学术交流能力的培养——一项基于"国际学术交流英语"课程的实证研究[J]. 中国ESP研究,2019,10(2):100-110,129.